PERSONALITY

THE SERIES IN CLINICAL AND COMMUNITY PSYCHOLOGY

CONSULTING EDITORS:

CHARLES D. SPIELBERGER and IRWIN G. SARASON

Averill	Patterns of Psychological Thought: Readings in Historical and Contemporary Texts
Becker	Depression: Theory and Research
Bermant, Kelman, and Warwick	The Ethics of Social Intervention
Brehm	The Application of Social Psychology to Clinical Practice
Cattell and Dreger	Handbook of Modern Personality Theory
Endler and Magnusson	Interactional Psychology and Personality
Friedman and Katz	The Psychology of Depression: Contemporary Theory and Research
Iscoe, Bloom, and Spielberger	Community Psychology in Transition
Janisse	Pupillometry: The Psychology of the Pupillary Response
Kissen	From Group Dynamics to Group Psychoanalysis: Therapeutic Applications of Group Dynamic Understanding
Klopfer and Reed	Problems in Psychotherapy: An Eclectic Approach
London	Personality: A New Look at Metatheories
Manschreck and Kleinman	Renewal in Psychiatry: A Critical Rational Perspective
Olweus	Aggression in the Schools: Bullies and Whipping Boys
Reitan and Davison	Clinical Neuropsychology: Current Status and Applications
Smoll and Smith	Psychological Perspectives in Youth Sports
Spielberger and Diaz-Guerrero	Cross-Cultural Anxiety
Spielberger and Sarason	Stress and Anxiety, volume 1
Sarason and Spielberger	Stress and Anxiety, volume 2
Sarason and Spielberger	Stress and Anxiety, volume 3
Spielberger and Sarason	Stress and Anxiety, volume 4
Spielberger and Sarason	Stress and Anxiety, volume 5
Ulmer	On the Development of a Token Economy Mental Hospital Treatment Program
	IN PREPARATION
Cohen and Ross	Handbook of Clinical Psychobiology and Pathology
Krohne and Laux	Achievement, Stress, and Anxiety

PERSONALITY
a new look at metatheories

Edited by

Harvey London
New School for Social Research

With an Introduction by

NANCY HIRSCHBERG
University of Illinois at Chicago Circle

HEMISPHERE PUBLISHING CORPORATION

Washington London

A HALSTED PRESS BOOK
JOHN WILEY & SONS

New York London Sydney Toronto

Hemisphere Publishing Corporation
1025 Vermont Ave., N.W., Washington, D.C. 20005

Distributed solely by Halsted Press, a Division of John Wiley & Sons, Inc., New York

1 2 3 4 5 6 7 8 9 0   D O D O   7 8 3 2 1 0 9 8

Library of Congress Cataloging in Publication Data
Main entry under title:

Personality: a new look at metatheories.

(The Series in clinical and community psychology)
Includes bibliographical references and indexes.
1. Personality. 2. Personality—Research.
I. London, Harvey.
BF698.P358   155.2   78-7022
ISBN 0-470-26381-4

Printed in the United States of America

To Kurt Lewin

The psychologist who, among the first, probably most forcefully brought to our attention the interaction between the person and his/her environment

CONTENTS

PREFACE

The experimental approach to the study of personality is in a state of crisis. One might argue that similar statements hold true for a number of areas of psychology, but it seems truer of the field of personality. In the first place, Walter Mischel[1] has argued firmly that there is less stability of characteristics among persons than was formerly supposed. In the second place, even if one were to assume stability, a sampling of personality texts would reveal coverage of topics that have nothing to do with stability of characteristics among persons, in turn revealing a poor understanding among personality psychologists of what their field is all about. Finally, in surveying the work on stable characteristics,[2] one finds neither reason nor structure to the characteristics that have been chosen for study. This last point indicates that there is no guiding principle, no direction, at work in the field.

In response to these difficulties, the contributors to this book have attempted some metatheoretical spadework. We have asked a number of questions, among them: How is a trait to be properly understood? How might a unified theory of personality be brought about? Are there assumptions underlying Mischel's work that need clarification?

We present a number of essays on such topics, essays that

[1] Mischel, W. *Personality and assessment.* New York: Wiley, 1968.

[2] London, H., and Exner, J. E., Jr. *Dimensions of personality.* New York: Wiley, in press.

we believe will clarify some of the fuzzy issues in experimental personality research. The book is intended for all serious students of the philosophy and theory of personality. It also can be of use to investigators in allied fields. There is a coherence to the book, but it is a loose coherence; chapters do not neatly follow one another.

I would like to thank the following people for their special contributions to this volume: Nancy Hirschberg, professor of psychology, University of Illinois at Chicago Circle; Florence Geis, associate professor of psychology, University of Delaware; and David Schneider, professor of psychology, University of Texas at San Antonio.

Harvey London

INTRODUCTION

According to one of Bertrand Russell's theories, an object is nothing but the totality of views, actual and possible, of that object. Our perception of a chair, for example, depends on our looking at the chair from different heights, distances, and angles. The composite of all of these actual, single viewings as well as of all potential viewings constitutes the object. If the subject matter of personality is, like Russell's object of perception, the composite of perspectives presented in this volume, one gets a very curious picture of the field. For here we have a collection of papers presenting a variety of original and interesting but very different theoretical views of the discipline.

Each paper has a definite bias in characterizing the field of personality. The authors disagree about the importance of mental experience, the need for theory, and the type of construct that should command attention in personality research. The only point on which the papers agree is that personality research has failed to fulfill its early promise to explain and predict behavior. Each paper offers a different solution to this problem.

On one side are Fiske and London, both of whom urge that personality be confined to the study of a few consensually validated constructs. London would like to see a panel of eminent personality psychologists decide which traits those in the field should study. Fiske, on the other hand, forecasts that personality will become a science only by confining itself to the study of a set of objectively measurable constructs that have a physical basis. On the other side of the issue are Hirschberg and Mischel. Basing her views on a logical analysis of the meaning of personality trait constructs, Hirschberg urges psychologists to make more, rather than fewer, distinctions among traits, while Mischel adds more cognitive variables to the growing list of constructs that he feels should replace personality traits. Mischel, whose ideas have set the stage for the next decade of personality research, here presents his growing concern with personality traits as viable constructs in behavioral prediction. He suggests not only that cognitive constructs are more fruitful variables for research, but also that new measurement methods must be found to replace our old paper-and-pencil measures of traits. These new measurement methods can be found in the work of the cognitive psychologists.

Mischel is not the only contributor to this volume who stresses the importance of the way in which people respond cognitively to the environment. Both Golding and Geis argue that cognitive systems should play a critical role in the study of personality. Golding introduces the concept of a "psychological organizing principle" and operationally defines it as the way in which people interpret and respond to their external world. By arguing that physical reality depends on someone's interpretation of it, Golding attacks the assumption underlying the trait-versus-situation controversy, for the extreme form of that controversy assumes an objectively measurable world that is not subject to individual differences in interpretation. Geis, too, takes the position that what explains the observer's behavior is not the external situation alone but the external situation as interpreted by an observer. Both Geis and Golding argue that a theory of the relationship between personality traits and behavior must include a construct involving the interpretation of the situation in which the behavior occurs.

Christie sees the relationship between personality traits and behavior as the major issue in personality research. He presents a case history of research in Machiavellianism to illustrate his notion that behavioral correlates of personality traits can be found in the laboratory, given a deep understanding of the trait as well as a theoretical analysis of the situational constraints on the behavior of interest.

The measurement methods and models favored by the authors are, of course, dependent on the constructs they emphasize. To measure psychological organizing principles, Golding resurrects the interview in the form of a structured, interactive session with trained observers. As an integral part of the interview, people are asked to comment on videotapes of their own interactions; in this way, according to Golding, they reveal their perceptions of their own motives, thoughts, principles, and characters. On the behavioristic side, Fiske argues that personality data, to be scientific, should be confined in space and time. Rather than obtain measures of sociability, the experimenter is urged to use trained observers to rate behaviors having a physical referent: laughs, smiles, nods, and gazes. Christie's interests lie with the objectively scored, self-report personality test of Machiavellianism, defined as a concern with the manipulation of other persons.

More mentalistic is Mischel's reliance on introspection. If we want to measure a person's motives, traits, or personal cognitions, we treat the person as an expert and ask him or her. More important to Mischel's thesis is the idea of constructing a taxonomy of situations, which, in turn, depends on the measurable properties of the situations. Possible situational variables are offered that lend themselves to measurement, such as population density, furniture arrangement, and temperature. Unlike Golding and Geis, Mischel does not assume that there are important individual differences in the interpretation of the physical world. In contrast to Golding and Mischel, Geis argues that the determinants of an individual's interpretation of a situation often operate below the threshold of conscious awareness, so that questioning a person directly does not always yield accurate measures of personality constructs. Although the determinants may be inaccessible to direct measurement, their effects on the subject's behavior can be detected on the basis of the way in which an observer reacts to the subject. Christie's paper explores the reasons underlying the failure of tests and behavior to correlate. Christie's penetrating analysis and review of the research relating personality tests and behavior suggest that behavior can be predicted by a test only if aspects of the situation relevant to the elicitation of the personality trait are present during the experiment. It is left to the experimenter's ingenuity and imagination to manipulate those situational features that interact with the behavior of interest.

London, noting the importance of the interaction between personality traits and physiological states, would like to see physiological measures assume a more central role in personality theory. Hirschberg adds beliefs and desires to the theoretical network of personality constructs and uses the measurement methods found in decision theory as an appropriate model for personality. Hirschberg also exhorts the reader to consider measurement models that allow the detection of individual differences in personality traits, beliefs, desires, and intentions. Such models are based on the analysis of types, or subgroups, of individuals, and the models can be equally well applied to the study of situations when the important situational parameters can be measured.

Each paper in this volume is self-contained, presenting a partisan view of personality. If, upon reading the volume, the reader questions the possibility of having a coherent science of personality, he or she is reminded of Fiske's proposal: that the study of personality be broken up into a set of separate disciplines, each with its own constructs and measurement models. Each subdiscipline of personality would be its own miniscience, contributing to the other subdisciplines but not depending on them.

Another conclusion the reader might reach is that the subject matter of personality can be seen from a number of different perspectives, as many, in fact, as there are theorists. The whole of personality, like Russell's objects, is a composite of all possible (actual and potential) perspectives. This view of personality is reminiscent of one of George Kelly's notions:

> For example, it has long been customary and convenient to distinguish between "mental" and "physical" facts. These are two artificially distinguished realms, to which two types of construction systems are respectively fitted; the psychological construction system and the natural science group of constructions systems. It is becoming increasingly clear, however, that we have on our hands two alternative construction systems, which can both be applied profitably to an ever increasing body of the same facts. The realms overlap.[1]

Nancy Hirschberg

[1] Kelly, George A. *A theory of personality: The psychology of personal constructs.* New York: Norton, 1955, p. 10.

PERSONALITY

PERSONALITY RESEARCH: A LOOK AT THE FUTURE

WALTER MISCHEL
Stanford University

My look at the future of personality research begins with a look at the past: What are some of the main lessons we have learned, or should have learned, from previous experience?

MULTIPLE DETERMINISM OF BEHAVIOR AND CONTEXTUALISM

For me, one of the most impressive, and obvious, lessons from the history of personality research is the recognition that

This paper (in slightly modified form) was published under the title "On the future of personality measurement" in the *American Psychologist,* 1977, *32,* 246–254. Copyright 1977 by the American Pyschological Association. Reprinted by permission.

Preparation of this chapter was facilitated by Grant MH 6830 from the National Institute of Mental Health and by Grant HD MH 09814 from the National Institute of Child Health and Human Development.

complex human behavior tends to be influenced by many determinants, and that it reflects the almost inseparable and continuous interaction of a host of variables both in the person and the situation. In the abstract, this recognition seems as bland and obvious as a cliché, and one wonders if a focus on interactionism and multiple determinism may not be little more than the substitution of new slogans for old verities. But when examined more concretely, this recognition has deeper implications that I sense are being felt independently in other areas of psychology and even in other social sciences.

Implicit in this recognition is that, if human behavior is determined by many interacting variables, both in the person and in the environment, then a focus on any one of them is likely to lead to limited predictions and generalizations. This recognition of the limits of prediction is not confined to the area of personality psychology. The same conclusion has been reached in analyses of topics as diverse as the effects of interview styles in psychotherapy, the impact of teaching practices and classroom arrangements in education, and the role of instructions to aid recall in memory experiments (Mischel, 1976). For example, after a survey of research on memory, Jenkins (1974) cautioned: "What is remembered in a given situation depends on the physical and psychological context in which the event was experienced, the knowledge and skills that the subject brings to the context, the situation in which we ask for evidence for remembering, and the relation of what the subject remembers to what the experimenter demands" (p. 793). The sentence would be equally apt if we substituted action for memory: Thus, what is done (or thought, or felt) in a given situation depends on the physical and psychological context in which the event is experienced, the knowledge and skills that the subject brings to the context, the situation in which we ask for evidence, and so on. Identical conclusions probably would be reached for the subject matter of any other subarea of psychology and perhaps throughout the social sciences. Hence, it becomes difficult to achieve broad, sweeping generalizations about human behavior; many qualifiers (moderators) must be appended to our "laws" about cause-and-effect relations almost without exception and perhaps with no exceptions at all (Cronbach, 1975).

Specificity (or "contextualism," to use Jenkins's phrase) may occur because of the large range of different ways that different people may react to the "same" treatments and reinterpret them (e.g., Cronbach, 1975; Neisser, 1974) and because the impact of most situations usually can be changed easily by coexisting conditions (Mischel, 1974). Thus, even a relatively simple stimulus or situation may produce a variety of often unpredictable specific (and weak) effects, depending on a large number of moderating variables and the many different ways in which the particular "subjects" may view them and transform them.

I want to stress that the fact that the details of context—or, if you will, of the situation—crucially affect behavior is as true when one wants to understand how a sentence is recognized or how a geometric pattern is identified as it is in the more global domain of personality psychology. Colleagues in such areas as cognition, memory, and psycholinguistics are discovering, just as we have, the limits of the generalizations they can achieve and the necessity of taking full account of context in their theorizing (e.g., Bransford & Johnson, 1973). The problems of our area may be more dramatic, but they are not unique.

While the more modest, carefully circumscribed goals and the predictive limitations implied by these conclusions appear to depress and discourage some social scientists (e.g., Cronbach, 1975; Fiske, 1974, Chap. 2), I do not share such gloom. On the contrary, more limited, specific, modest goals may be refreshing for a field in which hubris has often exceeded insight. The need to qualify generalizations about human behavior complicates life for the social scientist, but it does not prevent us from studying human affairs scientifically; it only dictates a respect for the complexity of the enterprise and alerts us to the dangers of oversimplifying the nature and causes of human behavior. It should be plain that this danger is equally great whether one is searching for generalized (global) person-free situational effects or for generalized (global) situation-free personality variables. In the context of personality measurement, a serious recognition of multiple determinism and interactions has many specific implications, and I want to consider a few of them now.

MULTIPLE GOALS FOR PERSONALITY PSYCHOLOGY

A continuing source of confusion in the area of personality psychology is the failure of investigators to specify clearly the goals, purposes, or objectives of their particular enterprise. It is perfectly legitimate, interesting, and appropriate to study what "people are like" (in general), if one is interested in such person perceptions; likewise, it is equally valid to study what "people will do" (in specific situations), if one is interested in that question. Each goal requires different strategies and provides somewhat different–albeit complementary, one hopes–insights. But there is no reason to think that one will substitute for the other. The value of each depends at least in part on the investigator's purposes and the types of generalizations sought.

It is easy to forget that one may construe the study of persons alternatively from many complementary perspectives, as the diverse papers in this volume illustrate. From the viewpoint of the psychologist seeking strategies to induce changes in performance, it may be most useful to focus on the environmental *conditions* or situations required to modify behavior, and therefore to speak of stimulus control, operant conditioning, classical conditioning, counter-conditioning, reinforcement control, modeling, and the like. From the perspective of the theorist interested in how these operations produce their effects in the individual who undergoes them, it may be more useful to focus on competencies, constructs, expectancies, subjective values, rules, and other theoretical *person variables* that mediate the effects of conditions upon behavior (Mischel, 1973). From the viewpoint of the perceiver, it may be more useful to characterize the inferred qualities of the individual in terms of *trait attributes* described with everyday adjectives. From the viewpoint of the experiencing subject, it may be more useful to search for the *phenomenological impact* of events, focusing on affects, thoughts, wishes, and other subjective (but communicable) internal states of experience. Confusion arises when one fails to recognize that the same events (e.g., the desensitization of a client's anxieties) may be alternatively construed from each of these perspectives and that the choice of constructions and of measures depends on the construer's purpose. I do not believe (as does Fiske, Chap. 2) that we need multiple sciences of personality, but I do believe that we need multiple routes of personality research within the same larger science and trust that ultimately conceptualizations in the field of personality will become able to encompass and integrate the phenomena seen from such multiple perspectives.

In sum, different goals require different foci and measurement and research strategies, all of which may be legitimate routes for moving toward one's particular objectives. For a more concrete illustration, consider, for example, the old but often forgotten differences between norm-centered and person-centered measurement. Traditionally, most attention in personality measurement has been devoted to comparing differences between people on some norm, standard, or dimension selected by the assessor. Such a norm-centered approach compares people against each other, usually on a trait or attribute continuum such as amount of introversion–extraversion. The results can help with gross screening decisions, permit group comparisons, and answer many research questions. But a norm-centered objective obviously requires a different strategy than one which is person centered (Mischel, 1968).

With a person-centered focus, the investigator tries to describe the particular individual in relation to the particular psychological conditions of that person's life. In my view, some especially interesting recent developments have been of this type, arising from clinical work with troubled individuals in the real-life setting in which the behaviors of interest unfold naturally. While there are many methodological variations, the essence of the approach is a functional analysis that investigates in vivo covariations between changes in the individual and changes in the conditions of his or her life. The interest here is not in how people compare to others but in how they can move closer to their own goals and ideals if they change their behavior in specific ways as they interact with the significant people in their lives (e.g., Kelly, 1955; Mischel, 1968, 1976).

In this venture there are many challenges. Perhaps most important is the fact that clients, like other people, do not describe themselves with operational definitions. They invoke motives, traits, and other dispositions as ways of describing and explaining their experiences and themselves. Much of the assessor's task is to help clients in the search for such referents for their own personal constructs instead of forcing the assessor's favorite dispositional labels on them. Rather than leading clients to repackage their problems in our terms, with our constructs, we need to help them objectify their constructs into operational terms, so that the relevant behaviors can be changed by helping the clients achieve more judicious arrangements of the conditions in their lives. In my crystal ball gazing, the future of personality research will, it is hoped, include increasingly imaginative and effective versions of such person-centered functional analyses. When done well, such analyses not only can provide a helpful service to people who need it but also can simultaneously offer a testing ground for our theoretical notions about the basic rules that underlie behavior.

INTERACTIONS IN REAL-LIFE SETTINGS

Both conceptually and methodologically, such therapeutic efforts are closely related to the broader problems of analyzing both behavioral stability and change under in vivo conditions. In the future, energetic efforts should be directed increasingly toward the analysis of naturally occurring behaviors observed in the interactions among people in real-life settings. Traditionally, trait-oriented personality research has studied individual differences in response to the "same" situation, usually in the form of a standard set of test questions. However, some of the most striking differences between persons may be found, not by studying their responses to the same situation, but by analyzing their selection and construction of stimulus conditions. In the conditions of real life, the psychological stimuli that people encounter are neither questionnaire items nor experimental instructions nor inanimate events; rather, they involve people and reciprocal relationships (e.g., with spouse, with boss, with children). We are continuously influencing the situations of our lives as well as being affected by them in a mutual, organic interaction (e.g., Raush, Barry, Hertel, & Swain, 1974). Such interactions reflect not only our reactions to conditions but also our active selection and modification of conditions through our own choices, cognitions, and actions (Wachtel, 1973). Different people select different settings for themselves; conversely, the settings that people select may provide clues about their personal qualities (Eddy & Sinnett, 1973). The mutual interaction between person and conditions becomes evident when behavior is studied in the interpersonal contexts in which it is evoked, maintained, and modified.

The study of social interactions vividly reveals how each person continuously selects, changes, and generates conditions just as much as he or she is affected by them. The future of personality measurement will be brighter if we can move beyond our favorite pencil-and-paper and laboratory measures to include direct observation as well as unobtrusive nonreactive measures to study lives where they are really lived and not merely where the researcher finds it convenient to look at them. In such studies, striking individual differences in preferred situations—in the contexts, environments, and activities different people prefer and select—are sure to be found. Such findings might permit profiles of high- and low-frequency situations and high- and low-frequency behaviors, somewhat like those supplied by interest inventories.

SUBJECTS AS EXPERTS AND COLLEAGUES

While direct observation is essential for the ecologically valid study of stability and change, I am equally impressed by another point that seems to be emerging from many different research directions; namely, our subjects are much smarter than many of us thought they were. Hence, if we do not stop them by asking the wrong questions and if we provide appropriate structure, they often can tell us much about themselves and indeed about psychology itself (see Golding, Chap. 4).

In some recent pilot work, for example, Harriet Nerlove Mischel and I asked young children what they know about psychological principles—about how plans can be made and followed most effectively, how long-term work problems can be organized, how delay of gratification can be mastered. We also asked them to tell us about what helps them to learn and (stimulated by Flavell and his colleagues, e.g., Kreutzer, Leonard, & Flavell, 1975) to remember. Although our results are still tentative, we have been impressed by how much even an 8-year-old knows about mental functioning. Indeed, one wonders how well such young children might perform on a final exam in introductory psychology if the jargon and big words were stripped away. (I do not want to imply, incidentally, that psychology knows little; rather, I believe people are good psychologists and know a lot. We professionals might be wise to enlist that knowledge in our enterprise.)

The moral for me is that it would be wise to allow our subjects to slip out of their roles as passive assessees or testees and to enroll them, at least sometimes, as active colleagues who are the best experts on themselves and are eminently qualified to participate in the development of descriptions and predictions, not to mention decisions, about themselves. Of course, if we want individuals to tell us about themselves directly, we have to ask questions that they can answer. If we ask people to predict how they will behave on a future criterion (e.g., job success, adjustment) but do not inform them of the specific criterion measure that will constitute the assessment, we cannot expect them to be accurate. Similarly, it might be possible to use self-reports and self-predictions more extensively in decision making, such as to help the person "self-select" from a number of behavioral alternatives (e.g., different types of therapy, different job assignments). Such applications would require conditions in which people's accurate self-reports and honest choices could not be used against them. We might, for instance, expect job candidates to predict correctly which job they will perform best, but only when all the alternatives available to them in their choice are structured as equally desirable. We cannot expect people to deny themselves options without appropriate alternatives.

Self-reports will always be constrained by the limits of the individual's own awareness. Too often, however, it has been assumed that people were unaware when in fact they were simply being asked the wrong questions. In the context of verbal conditioning, for example, more careful inquiries suggest that subjects may be far more aware than we thought (e.g., Spielberger & DeNike, 1966). Similarly, while a belief in the prevalence of distortions from unconscious defenses such as repression is the foundation of the commitment to an indirect-sign approach in assessment, the experimental evidence for the potency of such mechanisms remains remarkably tenuous (e.g., Mischel, 1976). And in laboratory research into unconscious responding (e.g., Eriksen, 1960), just as in the context of personality testing, what the person tells us directly generally turns out to be as valuable an index as any other more indirect sign (e.g., galvanic skin response).

One demonstration of the wisdom of enlisting the subject's self-knowledge to increase predictive power is the recent Bem and Allen (1974) study. Fully recognizing the "discriminativeness" that people so often display, Bem and Allen proposed that consistency may characterize *some* people at least in *some* areas of behavior. They suggested that while some people may be consistent (maintaining their position relative to others) on some traits, practically nobody is consistent on all traits; indeed, many traits that are studied by investigators may be completely irrelevant for many of the people who are studied. To get beyond this problem, Bem and Allen tried to identify those college students who would be consistent and those who would not be consistent on the traits of friendliness and conscientiousness. Their hypothesis was this: "Individuals who identify themselves as consistent on a particular trait dimension will in fact be more consistent cross-situationally than those who identify themselves as highly variable" (Bem & Allen, 1974, p. 512). On the whole, their results supported the hypothesis, demonstrating consistency for "some of the people some of the time." To me it is most interesting that it was the people themselves who predicted their own consistency, again providing support for the notion that each person knows his or her own behavior best.

The search for subtypes of people who display consistencies on some well-defined dimensions of behavior under some subtypes of conditions represents a more modest (and much more reasonable) search for personality typologies. Of course, the demonstration of such consistencies would not mean that the individuals did not discriminate among situations in their behavior, but it would indicate that they maintained their expected position relative to others with regard to certain types of behavior under certain types of conditions. Consistency in personality need not imply sameness, but it does imply a degree of predictability based on the individual's qualities. To the extent that such typologies are carefully qualified and take account of types of situations as well as types of people, they are likely to be more successful, albeit more limited, than their more global and ambitious ancestors.

ANALYSIS OF ENVIRONMENTS

In the future, many of us are sure to continue searching for cross-situationally consistent types of people, but others seem to be focusing increasingly on the social and psychological environments in which people live and function. The dramatic rise of interest in the environment as it relates to the person is documented easily; from 1968 to 1972 more books appeared on the topic of man–environment relations from an ecological perspective than had been published in the preceding three decades (Jordan, 1972). As is true in most new fields, a first concern in the study of environments is to try to classify them into a taxonomy. Environments, like all other events, of course, can be classified in many ways, depending mainly on the purposes and imagination of the classifiers. One typical effort to describe some of the almost infinite dimensions of environments, proposed by Moos (1973, 1974), calls attention to the complex nature of environments and to the many variables that can characterize them. Those variables include the weather, the buildings and settings, the perceived social climates, and the reinforcements obtained for behaviors in a particular situation, to list just a few.

The classification alerts us to a fact that has been slighted by traditional trait-oriented approaches to personality: Much human behavior depends delicately on environmental considerations, such as the setting (e.g., Barker, 1968), and even on such specific physical and psychosocial variables within that setting as how hot and crowded the setting is, how the room and furniture are arranged, or how the people in the setting are organized (e.g., Krasner & Ullmann, 1973; Moos & Insel, 1974). Many links between characteristics of the environment and behavior have been demonstrated. For example, measures of population density (such as the number of people in each room) may be related to certain forms of aggression, even when social class and ethnicity are controlled (Galle, Gove, & McPherson, 1972). Likewise, interpersonal attraction and mood are negatively affected by extremely hot, crowded conditions (Griffitt & Veitch, 1971).

Depending on one's purpose, many different classifications are possible and useful (e.g., Magnusson & Ekehammar, 1973; Moos, 1973, 1974). To seek any single basic taxonomy of situations may be as futile as searching for a final or ultimate taxonomy of traits, for we can label situations in at least as many different ways as we can label people. It will be important to avoid emerging simply with a trait psychology of situations, in which events and settings, rather than people, merely are given different labels. The task of naming situations cannot substitute for the job of analyzing *how* conditions and environments interact with the people in them.

Although person-condition interactions are never static, sometimes environmental variables can be identified that help to explain continuities in behavior and allow useful predictions. Of course, the psychology of personality cannot ignore the person; nevertheless, behavior sometimes may be predicted and influenced efficaciously from knowledge of powerful stimulus conditions (Mischel, 1968). The value of predictions based on knowledge of stimulus conditions is illustrated, for instance, in efforts to predict the posthospital adjustment of mental patients. Such investigations have shown that the type, as well as the severity, of psychiatric symptoms displayed depends significantly on environmental conditions, with little consistency in behavior across changing situations (Ellsworth, Foster, Childers, Arthur, & Kroeker, 1968). Accurate predictions of posthospital adjustment require knowledge of the environment in which the former patient will be living in the community, such as the availability of jobs and family support, rather than on any measured person variables or on in-hospital behavior (e.g., Fairweather, 1967; Fairweather, Sanders, Cressler, & Maynard, 1969). Likewise, to predict intellectual achievement, it also helps to take account of the degree to which the child's environment supports (models and reinforces) intellectual development (Wolf, 1966). And when powerful treatments are developed, such as modeling and desensitization therapies for phobias, predictions about outcomes are best when based on knowledge of the treatment to which the individual is assigned (e.g., Bandura, Blanchard, & Ritter, 1969). In the same vein, the significance of the psychological situation was vividly demonstrated in the simulated prison study conducted by Haney, Banks, and Zimbardo (1973).

ANALYSIS OF PERSON VARIABLES

When relevant situational information is absent or minimal, when predictions are needed about individual differences in response to the same conditions, or when situational variables are weak, information about person variables becomes essential. Moreover, a psychological approach requires that we move from descriptions of the environment—of the climate, buildings, social settings, and so forth, in which we live—to the psychological processes through which environmental conditions and people influence each other reciprocally. For this purpose, it is necessary to study in depth how the environment influences behavior and how behavior and the people who generate it in turn shape the environment in an endless interaction. To understand the interaction of person and environment we must consider person variables as well as environmental variables.

The person variables that in my view demand more research in the future must subsume such cognitive work as information processing with all its many ramifications. These variables include selective attention and encoding, rehearsal and storage processes, cognitive transformations, and the active construction of cognitions and actions (Bandura, 1971; Mischel, 1973; Neisser, 1967). Elsewhere, I proposed a synthesis of seemingly promising constructs about persons, developed in the areas of cognition and social learning (Mischel, 1973), which I called "cognitive social learning person variables." The constructs I selected were intended to be suggestive and constantly open to progressive revisions. I did not expect these variables to provide ways to predict accurately broad cross-situational behavioral differences between persons. In my view, the discriminativeness of behavior and its unique organization within each person are facts of nature, not limitations specific to particular theories. It is my hope that these variables may suggest useful ways of conceptualizing and studying specifically how the qualities of the person influence and even transform the effects of stimuli (environments, situations, treatments) and how each person generates distinctive, complex behavior patterns in interaction with the conditions of his or her life.

To summarize very briefly: First, individuals differ in their cognitive and behavioral *construction competencies,* that is, in their competence or ability to generate desired cognitions and response patterns. Second, differences in behavior may also reflect differences in how individuals *categorize* a particular situation. Obviously, people differ in how they encode, group, and label events and in how they construe themselves and others. Performance differences in any situation depend on differences in *expectancies* and specifically on differences in the expected outcomes associated with particular response patterns and stimulus configurations. Third, differences in performance may also be due to differences in the subjective *values* of the expected outcomes. And finally, individual differences often may reflect differences in the *self-regulatory systems and plans* that each individual brings to the situation. The study of this latter person variable will require analyses of the rules people use to guide their own behavior and investigation of how people pursue their long-term goals and how they select and transform stimulus conditions.

INTERFACE OF PERSONALITY AND COGNITION

Toward Grammars for People

I hope that in the future there will be an increasing awareness and fertile exploration of the many close parallels between the study of personality and of cognitive psychology. I believe that personality measurement, and personality psychology more generally, can benefit directly from the methods being developed by cognitive psychologists and, in turn, can enrich their work. Earlier in this chapter I noted the parallel between the discovery (or rediscovery) of contextualism in both cognitive and personality psychology. That is only one of many common parallels, only one of many shared concerns and problems that should be amenable to similar strategies of theoretical and empirical analysis. Let us consider a few of the others.

Ultimately, the study of individuality will have to deepen our understanding of how people abstract the gist of each other and themselves, forming schemata, expectations, or other cognitive representations that serve guiding and simplifying functions, enabling them to distill essential features from the otherwise overwhelming flood of trivial behavioral tidbits that confront the "unprepared mind." A recognition of the need for such constructs as schemata, expectancies, scripts, frames, and so on is hardly novel (as several other chapters in this volume illustrate). Some especially promising beginnings in the use of such cognitive constructs come, in my view, from efforts to understand how people comprehend sentences, conversations, and stories (e.g., Bower, 1976). These and related undertakings (e.g., Abelson, 1975; Schank, 1975) suggest that an adequate approach to how people understand their world—including events, sentences, and people—will have to take account of how they organize information in meaningful, hierarchical, rule-guided ways. Even the understanding of simple stories, for example, may be guided by a kind of "grammar" that provides a framework of rules for organizing information so that it may be more easily comprehended and remembered. Likewise, an adequate approach to the understanding of a person may require the development of a grammar of the individual. Such a grammar, to be useful, would help to specify the organization and relations among diverse parts or components of the individual's actions and attributes, allowing one to understand his or her goal-directed patterns and transactions with the world in a coherent fashion. Ideally, an adequate grammar of the individual also would specify how person variables like those discussed in the preceding section are organized and interrelated.

Again, a search for such a structural approach to individuality is far from new; it has long been the enduring ambition of most serious personality theorists. But as one looks to the future, such a structural approach, guided by the methods for the analysis of human understanding that are beginning to be developed by our cognitive colleagues, appears to have a better chance of successful realization. This approach will somehow have to transform the fine-grained formal analyses of the sort modeled by the best psycholinguists and cognitive psychologists so that they fit the persistently complex, molar, multifaceted subject matter of the personality psychologist. To me, that prospect looks difficult, full of hazards, but highly challenging and well worth pursuing (e.g., Cantor & Mischel, 1977).

Toward a Research-based Image of the Individual

Traditionally, most theorists of personality have invoked a few concepts and stretched them to encompass all the phenomena of human individuality, including thought, feeling, and behavior. As a result, we have theories of personality built on a few body types, or on a handful of factors, or on simple conditioning and environmental contingencies, or on the vicissitudes of one or more favorite motives (sex, aggression, competence, achievement, dissonance, self-realization), or on a humanism that correctly emphasizes the humanity of people but too easily loses sight of (or perhaps interest in) its antecedents. The list is long but the strategy is the same. Take a few concepts and stretch them as far as possible. This may be a valuable exercise for theorists interested in defending their favorite concepts. For the teacher, it may provide a handy set of controversies in which any one set of obviously incomplete, fragmentary ideas may be sharply contrasted against any other, with each sure to be found sorely lacking in at least some crucial ways. But for the psychologist who seeks a cumulative science of psychology based on the incremental, empirical discoveries of the field rather than on the biases of theoreticians committed to defending their viewpoints, such a strategy leaves dreadful voids.

To help overcome these voids, a conception of personality is required that, at the least, is nourished broadly by the research of the field. The massiveness of available data and, of course, their frequent flaws make it possible to read them in many different ways. In my reading, however, a distinctive image of the human being does begin to emerge from empirical work on cognition and social behavior.

One strand of this research suggests that the individual generally is capable of being his or her own best assessor, that the person's self-statements and self-predictions tend to be at least as good as the more indirect and costly appraisals of sophisticated tests and clinicians (e.g., reviewed in Mischel, 1968, 1972). A related theme is that the individual's awareness of the contingencies in the situation—his or her understanding, not the psychologist's, of which behavior leads to which outcome—is a crucial determinant of the resulting actions and choices, including behavior in the classical and instrumental conditioning paradigms (as discussed in Bandura, 1974; Mischel, 1973). In the same vein, any given, objective stimulus condition may have a variety of effects, depending on how the individual construes and transforms it (e.g., Mischel, 1974).

While these research themes focus on the centrality of each individual's interpretations, there is also much evidence for the potency and regularity of the effects that may be achieved when the rules of behavior are applied—with the individual's full cooperation and by the individual—to achieve desired outcomes (e.g., Bandura, 1969). There is also considerable support for the fact that while consistencies surely exist within each person, they tend to be idiosyncratically organized (e.g., Bem & Allen, 1974), a circumstance that makes nomothetic comparisons on common traits difficult and that highlights the uniqueness that Allport (1937) has so long emphasized.

Taken collectively, these and related research themes suggest an emerging image of the human being that seems to reflect a growing synthesis of several theoretical influences in current personality psychology. It is an image that seems compatible with many qualities of both the behavioral and the cognitive approaches to personality and yet one that departs from each in some respects.

This image is one of the human being as an active, aware problem-solver, capable of profiting from an enormous range of experiences and cognitive capacities, possessed of great potential for good or ill, actively constructing his or her psychological world, and influencing the environment but also being influenced by it in lawful ways, even if the laws are difficult to discover and hard to generalize. It views the person as so complex and multifaceted as to defy easy classifications and comparisons on any single or simple common dimension, as multiply influenced by a host of interacting determinants, as uniquely organized on the basis of prior experiences and future expectations, and yet as rule-guided in systematic, potentially comprehensible ways that are open to study by the methods of science. It is an image that has moved a long way from the instinctual-drive-reduction models, the static global traits, and the automatic stimulus-response bonds of traditional personality theories. It is an image that highlights the shortcomings of all simplistic theories that view behavior as the exclusive result of any narrow set of determinants, whether these are habits, traits, drives, reinforcers, constructs, instincts, or genes, and whether they are exclusively inside or outside the person. It will be exciting to watch this image change as new research and theory alter our understanding of what it is to be a human being.

REFERENCES

Abelson, R. P. Concepts for representing mundane reality in plans. In D. G. Bobrow & A. Collins (Eds.), *Representation and understanding.* New York: Academic Press, 1975.

Allport, G. W. *Personality: A psychological interpretation.* New York: Holt, Rinehart & Winston, 1937.

Bandura, A. *Principles of behavior modification.* New York: Holt, Rinehart & Winston, 1969.

Bandura, A. *Social learning theory.* Morristown, N.J.: General Learning Press, 1971.

Bandura, A. Behavior theory and the models of man. *American Psychologist,* 1974, *29,* 859-869.

Bandura, A., Blanchard, E. B., & Ritter, B. Relative efficacy of desensitization and modeling approaches for inducing behavioral, affective, and attitudinal changes. *Journal of Personality and Social Psychology,* 1969, *13,* 173-199.

Barker, R. G. *Ecological psychology.* Stanford, Calif.: Stanford University Press, 1968.

Bem, D., & Allen, A. On predicting some of the people some of the time: The search for cross-situational consistencies in behavior. *Psychological Review,* 1974, *81,* 506-520.

Bower, G. H. *Comprehending and recalling stories.* Division 3 Presidential Address, presented at the meeting of the American Psychological Association, Washington, D.C., September 1976.

Bransford, J. D., & Johnson, M. K. Considerations of some problems of comprehension. In W. Chase (Ed.), *Visual information processing.* New York: Academic Press, 1973.

Cantor, N., & Mischel, W. Traits as prototypes: Effects on recognition memory. *Journal of Personality and Social Psychology,* 1977, *35,* 38–48.

Cronbach, L. J. Beyond the two disciplines of scientific psychology. *American Psychologist,* 1975, *30,* 116–127.

Eddy, G. L., & Sinnett, R. E. Behavior setting utilization by emotionally disturbed college students. *Journal of Consulting and Clinical Psychology,* 1973, *40,* 210–216.

Ellsworth, R. B., Foster, L., Childers, B., Arthur, G., & Kroeker, D. Hospital and community adjustment as perceived by psychiatric patients, their families, and staff. *Journal of Consulting and Clinical Psychology Monograph,* 1968, *32*(5, Pt. 2).

Eriksen, C. W. Discrimination and learning without awareness: A methodological survey and evaluation. *Psychological Review,* 1960, *67,* 279–300.

Fairweather, G. W. *Methods in experimental social innovation.* New York: Wiley, 1967.

Fairweather, G. W., Sanders, D. H., Cressler, D. L., & Maynard, H. *Community life for the mentally ill: An alternative to institutional care.* Chicago: Aldine, 1969.

Fiske, D. W. The limits of the conventional science of personality. *Journal of Personality,* 1974, *42,* 1–11.

Galle, O. R., Gove, W. R., & McPherson, J. M. Population density and pathology: What are the relations for man? *Science,* 1972, *176,* 23–30.

Griffitt, W., & Veitch, R. Hot and crowded: Influences of population density and temperature on interpersonal affective behavior. *Journal of Personality and Social Psychology,* 1971, *17,* 92–98.

Haney, C., Banks, C., & Zimbardo, P. Interpersonal dynamics in a simulated prison. *International Journal of Criminology and Penology,* 1973, *1,* 69–97.

Jenkins, J. J. Remember the old theory of memory? Well, forget it! *American Psychologist,* 1974, *29,* 785–795.

Jordan, P. A real predicament. *Science,* 1972, *175,* 977–978.

Kelly, G. A. *The psychology of personal constructs* (Vols. 1 & 2). New York: Norton, 1955.

Krasner, L., & Ullman, L. P. *Behavior influence and personality: The social matrix of human action.* New York: Holt, Rinehart & Winston, 1973.

Kreutzer, M., Leonard, C., & Flavell, J. An interview study of children's knowledge about memory. *Monographs of the Society for Research in Child Development,* 1975, *40*(1, Serial No. 159).

Magnusson, D., & Ekehammar, B. An analysis of situational dimensions: A replication. *Multivariate Behavioral Research,* 1973, *8,* 331–339.

Mischel, H. N., Mischel, W., & Hood, S. Q. The development of knowledge about self-control. Unpublished manuscript, Stanford University, 1978.

Mischel, W. *Personality and assessment.* New York: Wiley, 1968.

Mischel, W. Direct versus indirect personality assessment: Evidence and implications. *Journal of Consulting and Clinical Psychology,* 1972, *38,* 319-324.

Mischel, W. Toward a cognitive social learning reconceptualization of personality. *Psychological Review,* 1973, *80,* 252-283.

Mischel, W. Processes in delay of gratification. In L. Berkowitz (Ed.), *Advances in experimental social psychology* (Vol. 7). New York: Academic Press, 1974.

Mischel, W. *Introduction to personality* (2nd ed.). New York: Holt, Rinehart & Winston, 1976.

Moos, R. H. Conceptualizations of human environments. *American Psychologist,* 1973, *28,* 652-665.

Moos, R. H. Systems for the assessment and classification of human environments. In R. H. Moos & P. M. Insel (Eds.), *Issues in social ecology.* Palo Alto, Calif.: National Press Books, 1974.

Moos, R. H., & Insel, P. M. *Issues in social ecology.* Palo Alto, Calif.: National Press Books, 1974.

Neisser, U. *Cognitive psychology.* New York: Appleton-Century-Crofts, 1967.

Neisser, U. Review of "Visual information processing." *Science,* 1974, *183,* 402-403.

Raush, H. L., Barry, W. A., Hertel, R. K., & Swain, M. A. *Communication, conflict, and marriage.* San Francisco: Jossey-Bass, 1974.

Schank, R. C. The structure of episodes in memory. In D. G. Bobrow & A. Collins (Eds.), *Representation and understanding.* New York: Academic Press, 1975.

Spielberger, D. C., & DeNike, L. D. Descriptive behaviorism versus cognitive theory in verbal operant conditioning. *Psychological Review,* 1966, *73,* 306-326.

Wachtel, P. Psychodynamics, behavior therapy, and the implacable experimenter: An inquiry into the consistency of personality. *Journal of Abnormal Psychology,* 1973, *82,* 324-334.

Wolf, R. The measurement of environment. In A. Anastasi (Ed.), *Testing problems in perspective.* Washington, D.C.: American Council on Education, 1966.

2

COSMOPOLITAN CONSTRUCTS AND PROVINCIAL OBSERVATIONS: SOME PRESCRIPTIONS FOR A CHRONICALLY ILL SPECIALTY

DONALD W. FISKE
University of Chicago

Personality research pertains to the extensive area called personality. But what is included within that subject matter? Personality encompasses all the ways that people look at people. It includes the way one person sees another, the way novelists and biographers portray their characters, and the variety of ways that researchers in that area construe the topic.

There are, in fact, as many definitions of personality as there are people working on it. There is a plethora of global theories; recently, many minitheories also have been propounded. Yet, in spite of all these instances—all the conceptualizations and perceptions of professionals and nonprofessionals and the almost infinite number of verbal descriptions and interpretive statements—there is not a real science. There is no pervasive consensus on what is being studied and on how it should be construed and measured.

Each investigator starts with his or her own construals, or descriptions, of people. Every person is a scientist forming personal constructs and hypotheses, as George Kelly (1955) pointed out two decades ago. He was ahead of his time. Personality researchers appear to have carried over from their lay experience their individual constructs as a framework for their research activities. These are cosmopolitan, global constructs, which the individual applies without qualification, that is, without restriction to place or time.

Your constructs and mine have some overlap and some similarity; yet they are clearly not identical. I tolerate your constructs and you, I trust, tolerate mine. When you use a word to describe a person, I usually think that I know what you mean. Even when you invent a new dimension, I usually can recognize instances in my experience in which your construct could apply to someone. Once in a while, I may even add your construct to my catalogue of descriptors, just as I may find useful lay terms such as ego trip. But in my professional work, even if I use the same term as you do, my meaning for it will not be precisely the same as yours. When several people represent Murray's needs in questionnaires or rating forms, the representations do not covary in identical ways (Fiske, 1973).

I and you and everyone else continue to preserve and apply our constructs because a construct cannot be infirmed. We cannot have experiences that prove a construct wrong. If we do not find a construct useful, we may use it less often, or modify it, or even reinterpret our experience to make the construct fit.

Personality refers to the ways people perceive and interpret behavior. It refers to the attribution of characteristics to individuals or groups of individuals, characteristics that typically are applied without restriction to particular local circumstances or points in time. Each attribution is an observer-observed entity. The fact that you and I may make somewhat similar attributions about someone must not prevent us from recognizing that your attribution has its individualistic component that is different from my personal contribution to my attribution.

On the one hand, there is the vast domain of human behavior, the constant flow of actions and interactions (not to mention the continuing internal mental processes that go on day and night within me and, I assume, within you and within everyone else). On the other hand, we have the many different ways of perceiving and interpreting that behavior—the layperson's, the writers', the humanists', and the behavioral scientists', and the individual ways of each person within each of these groups. It is no wonder that we have such a diversity of research studies within the personality area. We have an embarrassment of riches, but much of our apparent wealth is fools' gold. We have never established that any of the coins ring true, that any of our concepts provide a structure leading to a consensual understanding of the phenomena we study.

TOWARD SCIENCES OF PERSONALITY

Personality is not yet a science. It is prescientific because it does not have the paradigm that Kuhn (1963) prescribes as a criterion for a science. While the term paradigm seems to be open to almost as many interpretations as personality (cf. Masterman, 1970), it seems clear that there is not yet a consensus among most researchers on such fundamentals as a set of constructs and their meanings. There even seems to be a wide range of opinions about what constitutes a science. But we must start somewhere. Let me propose a list of essential characteristics for a science, a list that admittedly is not exhaustive.

1. A science must have consensus, among those practicing it, on several matters:
   a. The phenomena and objects being studied.
   b. The aspects of these materials to be considered.
   c. Acceptable ways of studying these phenomena.
   d. Rules for thinking and talking about these phenomena.
2. These matters must be somewhat explicit.
3. There must be consensus on some concepts. This consensus must be demonstrated by agreement on some applications of these concepts to phenomena.
4. There must be consensus among qualified observers on some observations, on the raw material to which concepts and their interrelationships are applied.

That is part of my philosophy of science. While you and I may not agree, at least you will know the starting point on which the rest of this paper is based.

The heading for this section does not contain a typographical error. I believe the domain now labeled personality will probably have to be broken up into several distinct disciplines or sciences, each with its own subject matter, its own particular selective approach to human behavior. These will be proposed in a later section.

Units of Observation

Each science has to be built upon discrete, provincial observations. Each observation is provincial because it is confined to a particular place and a given time. Schematically, we can write a mapping sentence indicating the facets in each observation (cf. Guttman, 1970): At time T, observer O perceives and cognizes X with respect to phenomenon P occurring at a point in space S.

Each observation, each datum, must have a value assigned to it for each of the several facets (T, O, etc.). Each value will be one of the elements specified as an alternative within that facet. In personality research, we have not recognized the significance of these facets and, in each investigation, have tended to overlook one or more of them. For example, each personality observation is made at a point in time, yet we ignore that facet. We take the observation about someone as applicable over some unspecified duration of time extending from before the moment of observation to after. This expansive interpretation stems in part from the fact that most observations are not taken as applicable to the behavior of the person at the moment of observation. Thus, a rating ordinarily refers to our integrated recollection of prior observations of the person (perhaps with more recent experiences being given more weight). Even in systematic observation, the rating applies to some period of seconds or minutes, not a moment. Crudely summarizing over time, such ratings and other kinds of personality data are more reflections of the observer's attributing and judging processes than records of behavioral acts as they occur naturally.

Time blurring A clear example of this time blurring can be seen in ratings of psychological adjustment. The judgment that a person is neurotic does not mean that the individual adjusts badly every time in every situation. Rather, the judgment refers to impressions from a number of occasions on which the person coped poorly, ignoring the many long intervals in between. It is a global interpretation, summarizing over an extended period of time.

There is time blurring in most personality research. As Mischel (1969) has suggested, we construe people's behavior in terms of stable and enduring dispositions, neglecting the discontinuities and changes from time to time and from situation to situation. Our constructions of people are more stable than the people's behaviors actually are. We use cosmopolitan constructs to simplify the complexity of our experience with others.

To check on the prevalence of this time blurring, I examined a recent issue, picked randomly, of the *Journal of Personality.* The majority of studies reported in the issue correlated two sets of self-report observations. Each set referred to some period of time, such as the way the subject usually is; and the two sets of observations were made at different points in time, the interval ranging from several minutes to a much longer time period.

Observer blurring In most of those studies, each of the two sets of observations was produced by the same observer, the subject. While the investigators obviously were aware of this source, they typically reported without restricting the results to those observers (i.e., as though other, external observers would have made essentially the same observations if they were in a position to do so). The blurring of observations by self and external observers in an actual pooling of data from these two sources is rare, for investigators ordinarily recognize that the perspective of the subject is not interchangeable with that of the independent observer (cf. Geis, Chap. 6). A more common kind of observer blurring occurs when the subjects are observed by other people; yet the observers are treated as interchangeable even though the recorded observations of each observer contain unique variations.

An example of observer blurring can be seen in psychodiagnosis. A person may be judged neurotic by one professional observer and psychotic by another; the spouse, meanwhile, may insist that the person is perfectly normal. Even when observers are interpreting the same material, such as a projective protocol, they frequently disagree. When a diagnosis is recorded for administrative purposes, the range of opinions among those who have observed the person is not reported. Subsequently, the diagnosis may be treated as if it were independent of the observer who made it.

Cognition blurring For analytic reasons, it is worthwhile to construe another kind of blurring. In rating another person or in reporting about ourselves, we blend and combine a series of perceptions and cognitions, all as represented in our recollections. This cognition blurring is another way of thinking about time blurring. Going further, we can apply the notion of cognition blurring to the combining of observational data from different observers. In a sense, the cognitions of individual reporters are stirred together when we average their separate ratings.

Place blurring Another facet is the point in space where the observation is made. We know that most personality observations are made in the testing room, the laboratory, or the clinic. We also know that your laboratory does not look exactly like mine. And we are very much aware of the fact that all of these locales are highly atypical of the places in which most behavior occurs. Yet, we overlook this ecological facet.

Examination of a contemporary issue of the *Journal of Personality and Social Psychology* revealed that a preponderance of the personality studies reported had essentially S–R designs. There was an independent variable–a set of conditions or a manipulation by the experimenter–and a dependent variable based on observations reported by the subject or someone else. Of course, the subjects came to the experimenter's place to permit the observations to be made. In addition to the blurring of place, there was also a blurring of the objects in that space. The stimuli used by the experimenter were not considered as identifiably discrete things but as representative of a broader class of things.

In considering these facets, I am discussing representativeness, generalizability, and external validity but using different terms for heuristic purposes. We are all aware of these matters, although we prefer to keep them out of focus, to blur them. With respect to the blurring of place, we know that place or situation has other aspects that could be identified appropriately as separate facets. In particular, there is the relationship between the persons being observed and the circumstances in which they are placed. Why are the subjects there? Did they come voluntarily (cf. Rosenthal & Rosnow on *The Volunteer Subject,* 1975)? What is the task given to the observer? What is the exact wording of the instructions to the subjects and the instructions to the observer?

It should be pointed out that, in these studies, the degree of blurring of time is typically less than in the studies correlating two self-reports. The observer reports on perceptions that cover a few minutes, and the interval between presentation of stimuli and observation is ordinarily of similar magnitude. (Whereas the contrast between the sets of studies in the two journals was marked, several studies in the *Journal of Personality* also involved manipulations of some kind.)

The several kinds of blurring described here occur within personality research. Most of the blurring takes place in the way the investigator plans and collects measurements; some of it occurs in the way the respondents carry out the task set for them. All of it stems from the manner in which we all view personality in our everyday living.

Units of Analysis

In personality research, the unit of observation is sometimes taken as the unit of analysis. Unit of analysis here refers to the datum entered into the statistical analysis. When a subject or a diagnostician makes a rating on a disposition, that rating is often used directly in the subsequent analysis. As we have seen, such a rating incorporates time blurring by summarizing or integrating recollections of experiences that cover both long and short periods of time. There also may be other kinds of blurring, such as blending the place in which each experience occurred with other places of observations.

More commonly, the unit of analysis is an explicit summarizing or averaging over units of observation. This practice is consistent with our use of large concepts that do not refer to any one particular behavioral act but to a tendency in actions, with place unspecified. In observer-dependent data, we often combine or average several specific responses to obtain a score. For example, in self-report questionnaires, the responses to the several items are combined. Alternatively, we may average the ratings of several observers.

We do this averaging or summarizing to minimize the unique contribution of the separate item or the given observer. We are seeking general, comprehensive scores to match our global concepts. But what does the average represent? What does it estimate? The psychometrician will tell you that it estimates a population or universe score, the score that would be obtained if one could make all appropriate observations for the entire universe. For example, in their definitive monograph on generalizability, Cronbach, Gleser, Nanda, and Rajaratnam (1972) had universe score as a basic concept, that score being the average of all the measurements of the person that the investigator would like to make, but cannot, under all conditions appropriate to the concept. But who has ever spelled out in complete detail the nature of such a universe? It would be a fruitless pursuit, because most of the observations we would like to sample simply cannot be sampled. We do what we can, which is very different from what we would ideally do, but we blur that discrepancy.

We also keep out of focus the warnings of Loevinger (1965) that we have no populations of tests, items, or testing conditions, as classical psychometric theory requires. In other words, we average over a set of items, or over several observers, to estimate something, without being able to say what that something is. If we attempt to define the hypothetical population, we do so in vague, general terms. We never have access to it. We cannot enumerate all members in that hypothetical class.

GENERALIZABILITY THEORY AS PLACEBO

It is largely because our units of analysis are averages over explicit units of observation that we partake of generalizability theory. This theory should be equally applicable to the combining of experiences into a single observation, but those experiences are not available to be measured separately. We ingest generalizability theory because we feel better afterward, as with a good placebo, even though it does not treat the basic dysfunction. (The word analgesic might be used in this connection if only the fundamental difficulties in our reliance on observer-dependent data caused us the pain that they should.)

Generalizability theory was created because psychologists, including personality researchers, begin with a priori concepts. We have a concept, formulated from our personal experience or from the experience of our social group. We have a strong subjective conviction that it exists as an attribute of persons —and it does have an existence in our cognitive system for construing people. We want to measure it and we do the best we can, knowing implicitly or explicitly that the linkage between the concept and the measuring operation is weak and that the test is not a coordinating definition for the concept but only an approximation to it. Sociability exists; now let us see how good our test for sociability is. Sociability is a broad term covering a number of things, and so we decide we need several items to measure it. (Actually, there is a lot to be said for simply asking the subjects directly to rate themselves on sociability, as pointed out by Mischel, 1972, and brought out in Ashton and Goldberg, 1973, and in Jackson, 1975.)

If we use several items, however, we become concerned about whether they are measuring the same thing. There is a sound basis for this concern: such items typically correlate less than .10 with each other (e.g., Fiske, 1966). Nevertheless, we summarize over a large set of items and get a score that satisfies us because it correlates with the score from another set of items, actual or hypothetical.

Usually we do not make the painful mistake of measuring sociability in more than one way. We are satisfied with our test and see no need to add additional ones. Those who make that mistake are likely to be upset when they find that their several measures of sociability have only modest intercorrelations, sometimes in the range around .30 within which so many personality correlations fall, sometimes a little higher. With intercorrelations of that size, it is not surprising that the correlations between the score for sociability and the score for some other variable vary with the instrument being used to obtain the two scores (cf. Fiske, 1973).

We believe that a sociable person continues to be a sociable person and that our measurements of sociability should therefore be stable over time. We implicitly generalize from the moment of our observation to a range of other points in time, as the examination of reported research studies brought out.

Within generalizability theory, the crucial concern is validity. Reliability is important only in the service of validity. If our test is fully valid, we do not need to be concerned about reliability or even to investigate it. Among the several kinds of validity, face validity is rarely considered sufficient evidence. Criterion-oriented validity requires criterion measures in which one has more faith than one has in one's test. Construct validity is an elegant concept, capturing and making explicit the scientist's normal strategy for research programs. In practice, however, construct validity is rarely investigated in any intensive and comprehensive way in personality research because few personality concepts are embedded in explicit nomological nets specifying the positive, negative, and zero covariations that the construct is postulated to have with other constructs that are themselves adequately measured.

Whenever we study a concept induced from our experience—a cosmopolitan construct with an independent existence, not confined in space or time—we need whatever help we can get from generalizability theory. This is especially the case when our data are the attributions made by one person about another person. For contrast, consider the study of laughs, perhaps investigating whether the laugh of one person in a conversation is related temporally to the laugh of another. Here the unit of observation is the unit of analysis: Did a laugh occur at a particular moment? The concept of internal consistency is irrelevant for such a provincial observation as the occurrence of a laugh. Stability is not involved since we are not attributing a disposition to anyone. The only pertinent kind of reliability is agreement between observers: Do two or more observers agree closely on the moment when each laugh starts? Yes.

There need be no concern with validity of any kind. The

observation noting a laugh is the measurement we want; it is not an estimate of anything. To be sure, the design concepts of internal and external validity (Campbell & Stanley, 1963) apply to any study involving laughs. For the illustrative study concerning the sequencing of laughs by each participant, there would appear to be no difficulties with internal validity. External validity should be high if the protocols of laugh occurrences are obtained under reasonably naturalistic conditions.

Of course, the study of laughs or other acts is not concept free. Laughing, gazing, gesturing, and similar acts are concepts that come, for the most part, from everyday language and experience. They differ from the usual personality construct in being at a very low level of abstraction and closely linked to direct observations. In fact, each concept can be defined ostensively, indicating examples of the class and examples not of the class by simple pointing.

COSMOPOLITAN CONSTRUCTS AND FALLIBLE MEASUREMENTS

Personality researchers generally are optimistic about the possibility of making progress toward a science of personality as they see it. Their optimism is reinforced by the evidence of some regularities in their findings. (For example, some instruments yield similar sets of findings, provided that the tests are administered in the same way to two groups of subjects from the same population.) In reality, there is little hard evidence on which to base optimism. It is sobering and discouraging to examine carefully the field of personality research over the last 10, 20, or 30 years and try to find evidence of progress. What movement has there been toward agreement on concepts, on their definitions, or on standard procedures for assessing them? If, carrying out the proposal by London (Chap. 7), we could reach agreement, we might make a little progress.

A case probably can be made for progress in negative knowledge. We have learned that some lay beliefs are faulty (e.g., human judges cannot predict behavior better than actuarial models). We have established that people are not highly consistent over time and situations in their observed behaviors. The devastating critique of *Personality and Assessment* compiled by Mischel (1968) has been vigorously attacked but not refuted. More particularly, we have gathered many demonstrations showing the numerous sources of slippage in personality measurement and research: Rosenthal (1966) collated findings on experimenter effects; Rosenthal and Rosnow (1969, 1975) reviewed subject effects and other artifacts; Cronbach (1946, 1950) noted response sets in responding to questionnaires; Kuncel (1973), Kuncel and Fiske (1974), and Minor and Fiske (1976) explored the complex and varying processes in arriving at responses. Problems with ratings have been known for decades. Other examples could be added to this list.

What has become clear is that there is much slippage in measuring personality. The various kinds of blurring that take place in measurements contribute to the deficiencies. There is also a somewhat different perspective to consider. Each datum in personality research is subject to influence from a variety of factors; each response is complexly determined. In principle, this complexity should not be insurmountable. The sources of variance should be identifiable and the contribution of each should be measurable. The difficulty is that we have no baseline. We cannot take personality into the laboratory and study it under conditions that eliminate most of the sources of slippage. Subjects in the laboratory respond to the atypical situation in which they find themselves. Only a few influences on their behavior are eliminated or even kept constant over subjects.

Another aspect of the complexity is in the inconsistent contributions of the several sources of slippage. The average weight for a determinant of behavior varies with environment or situation. And such an average conceals the individual differences in the extent of that contribution for the various subjects.

Optimists have defended their hopefulness by pointing out that it has been possible to identify signals embedded in a large amount of noise, as in research on evoked potentials. In such work, a stimulus is presented many times and the essence, the contribution of that stimulus, is distilled from the recordings of the neural processes. Note that the stimulus is well controlled and that the system being studied can be approximately identified in space and time. Note also that such processes show relatively little adaptation or other trends over time. In personality, the stimulus is usually complex, it does not have a single effect, and the neural systems that process the input from the stimulus are diverse and cannot be traced with any assurance. Moreover, the input is operated on in various ways during the much longer time interval between presentation of the stimulus and observed, gross behavioral response. Finally, the process and the response tend to change over a series of repeated trials.

This information on slippage in personality measurement has been known for some time; no new empirical findings have been reported here. If the extent and sources of slippage have been recognized, why have personality researchers continued to work as they always have? I think that our habits of thought from everyday living have been carried over to our research and have received varying reinforcement in the latter context.

As discussed earlier, people construe (describe) other people in everyday terminology, and their language works reasonably well. When one person describes another to us, we generally think we understand what is being said. Similarly, when we think about someone's behavior, we can talk to ourselves in the vernacular. In both instances, our descriptive concepts work for us; they serve our purposes fairly well.

Similar ways of thinking go on in our professional activities. Someone writes about a concept (e.g., aggression, locus of control, or delay of gratification) and we feel we understand what is written. The concepts used in the rather undisciplined discipline of personality "satisfice." This term was coined by Herbert Simon (1955, 1967) to refer to the acceptance of merely adequate solutions in making a decision. Although any problem may have an ideal or optimal solution, human beings typically do not expend the effort necessary to identify it. In much problem solving and decision making, people examine alternatives sequentially. As soon as they find one that is satisfactory, they accept it rather than continue in the hope of identifying the optimal choice. The net utility of accepting a satisfactory solution is expected to be higher than the utility of expending greater energy and time to attain a better solution. So, in everyday conversation, common words satisfice; we do not take the time to search our vocabularies for less common but more precise descriptive terms. In personality, we find that everyday concepts satisfice much of the time. We know what they mean. They serve to verbalize our impressions of other people and their behavior.

Our reactions to empirical research findings are similar. When we read a research report, we usually feel we can accept what the investigator concludes. We may feel that nothing new has been reported because we can fit some of our experience to the written statements. The consequence of being easily satisficed is that we are too uncritical. If a finding in our own research or in the research of others seems reasonable, it satisfices. We do not critically examine the pertinent concepts to determine whether they have the precision required for scientific terms. We are not troubled about the sources of slippage in the data analyzed. For example, we read that internality is correlated with political conservatism. If we find that statement plausible, we do not stop to consider the fact that locus of control responses have been shown to be multifactorial and that conservatism seems also to be multifaceted. And does the finding of a correlation between self-report measures for these cosmopolitan constructs say anything about the covariation of these attributes as judged by peers?

SELF-REPORTS

Self-report procedures satisfice all too readily, even though they epitomize most of the difficulties and limitations in personality research today. In particular, they are known to be sensitive to many features of the place in which they are applied. Yet, we use them because they are convenient and economical. We also use them because they are suitable for the study of our cosmopolitan constructs. We can simply ask each subject two questions and then correlate the answers; for example, "How conservative are you?" and "Do you feel that you have control over what happens to you?" Of course, because we recognize the looseness of words, we may use a number of more specific questions, and we may have subjects choose among alternatives we give them to avoid having to interpret the words they use in their replies. Even so, the greater part of personality research deals with words, in spite of their lack of precision (cf. Mandler & Kessen, 1959; Fiske, 1971, 1974). Personality is largely a verbal science, not a quantitative science employing univocal symbols.

There is no reason why we should not have a discipline concerned with the verbal statements that people make about themselves and others, as long as it is explicitly just that. The ways that people overtly describe themselves, their inner experience, and their impressions of others have importance. But we must not assume that propositions established for self-reports necessarily apply to other domains. All of us recognize that our verbal statements about our feelings are often rather unsatisfactory representations of our current experience. More significant is the uncertain connection between behavioral acts and contemporary reports of perceptions. There is good reason to believe that what a person claims to perceive is only part of what determines that person's overt behavior. In fact, both the report and the action may stem from some unverbalized internal reaction.

STRATEGIES FOR RESEARCH

What should be prescribed for that chronically ill specialty, personality research? Researcher, know thyself! Know what you are doing. State what phenomena you are trying to understand. Work out and make explicit your basic axioms and assumptions. On balance, does the evidence support your assumptions? Are they based on intuitive generalizations from your experience as you have construed it? It has been said that a science progresses by questioning its assumptions.

It is my impression that many personality researchers have had as their implicit goal the understanding of their impressions and cognitions of people, themselves and others. I think that was an unverbalized objective for me for many years. Perhaps some progress can be made toward that goal by aiming first at more restricted targets.

I believe the topic of personality can best be approached by identifying several disciplines, each concerned with a specified set of phenomena. Such differentiation is analogous to the differentiation that Deese (1972) predicted for psychology as a whole. I hope, however, that the separate existence of the several disciplines in each domain does not inhibit their interaction and cross-fertilization. Once the phenomena pertinent to a discipline have been chosen, the appropriate strategy can be determined. The term sciences, used earlier in this chapter, may be appropriate if the separate fields of study are sufficiently distinct. In a previous paper (Fiske, 1974), I referred to such fields as sciences of personality; in another (Fiske, 1977), as personologies; and, still more recently, as strategies (Fiske, 1978). Time will tell what the appropriate term should be. It will also become clear, in the years ahead, what the territory of each discipline should be.

Verbalized Perceptions

A fundamental distinction must be made between personologies studying verbalized perceptions and attributions and those studying other acts. The first set relies primarily on the use of words. As such, it involves a different level of analysis than the set studying movements in time and space. Within the category of personologies involving attributions, a major personology is that for societal problems. Here the focus is on matters with which society (and many personality researchers) are deeply concerned: mental health, delinquency, personnel selection and classification in education and industry, and so forth. The focus is on judgments by natural raters, judgments that make a difference in people's lives. The concepts are provided by society. (For a longer discussion of this and other personologies, see Fiske, 1977; see also Fiske, 1978.)

Another personology involving attributions is the study of the attributing process itself. How do people form impressions and make attributions to others? This question is particularly important in the judgmental attributions so crucial in societal problems. While this personology should contribute much to the understanding of societal problems, it is better classified within the complementary set of personologies where the investigator determines the problem, the class to be considered next.

Within this class, one personology might study the cognitive-social-learning person variables, which Mischel (1973, 1977) recently delineated. These include the person's cognitive and behavioral construction competencies, encoding strategies and personal constructs, subjective stimulus values, and self-regulatory systems and plans. Insofar as these refer to how a person processes the information in each particular situation, they do not fall under the rubric of trait or similar long-term dispositions. These variables are seen as topics for investigation in our efforts to understand the interaction between a person and a situation.

The same (or a closely related) personology might study the psychological organizing principles considered by Golding (Chap. 4) with emphasis on the construal styles of individuals. The success of that enterprise will depend upon the possibility of obtaining data that do not depend on the way each person uses words or upon the development of nomothetic constructs shared by researchers and tied explicitly to observables.

In this general personology, the concepts are not taken over from our everyday language and hence are more likely than most personality concepts to be modified as empirical data and findings demand. Note also that for many of Mischel's person variables, the content of the subject's construing—the expectancies, personal constructs, and so on—comprises the phenomena being studied, but the classification and dimensionality of that content are determined by the experimenter. This approach is similar to that of George Kelly (1955), in which nomothetic variables (e.g., permeability) are used to analyze personal constructs. It does seem essential to keep separate the construing done by persons and the constructs utilized by the scientist.

Discrete Acts

Very different from the preceding personologies is the personology concerned with acts, particularly those acts observable in conversations and other interactions between people. Examples of acts are gazes, smiles, gestures, and interruptions. The distinctive and contrasting features of this level of analysis are several. The protocols can be obtained under fairly naturalistic conditions. Words have at most a secondary role in this discipline. The datum is an act in a place at a point in time (recall the hypothetical study of laugh sequences in an earlier section). The coder indicates the locus of the act on the time scale, so that its behavioral context, its position in the sequence of other acts, can be determined. For data on acts, the only potential blurring appears to be that over observers, and this can readily be detected. Empirical data show very high levels of agreement between observers in their observational recordings of individual acts. Finally, these acts have the advantage of usually being in the periphery rather than the center of attention for both actor and perceiver.

This personology studies the processes of behaving as a sequence of acts, the acts of one person having contingent relationships to those of the other (e.g., Duncan, 1972, 1974). The unit of observation is usually the onset or the termination of each act—both apparently having information value. In some instances, an ongoing act, such as gesturing, is related to the occurrence or nonoccurrence of acts by the other person.

The strategy in this personology is to concentrate on these provincial observations, acts in their place and time, with the aim of determining their sequential relationships with other acts. What are the pertinent acts? What acts are related to the occurrence of acts by the other person? To what signals do these acts belong? What are the conventions and rules for interactions? Once some answers to these have been obtained, we can consider the particular individual's strategies in interactions. Where rules have alternatives, do individuals show simple preferences for some alternatives? In other instances where the system provides options, does the individual exercise them frequently or rarely and under what conditions? To what extent are the individual's strategies stable across interactions, with other people, in other situations, and so on?

A large study (Duncan & Fiske, 1977) provides a revealing contrast between two strategies for studying these acts. For each of 88 conversations, several dozen act scores were obtained for each participant by going back over the videotapes a number of times. Each score summarized a person's behavior in one type of act (e.g., for smiling there was a score for the number of smiles and also scores for the extent of smiling while not speaking). The intercorrelations among these scores produced modest results—some findings of interest but relatively few among the many possible relationships. The correlations with partner scores also were not particularly promising: Again, there were significant associations but the results as a whole were not very illuminating. Finally, these scores were correlated with several dozen scores from self-descriptive instruments for self and partner and with reactions reported after the conversations. Even less of deep significance was uncovered.

Acts in these and some other conversations were also examined in terms of their positions relative to other acts. In these analyses, it was possible to find a number of striking regularities, which were conceptualized as a system for speaking turns. In this system, the concepts were based on what was observed, the lowest level concepts being the acts, and the concepts at a higher level being explicitly defined in terms of the lower level concepts. Within the turn system, a turn-yielding signal, a speaker-state signal, a speaker within-turn signal, and an auditor back-channel signal were discovered. These appear to be part of the structure within which conversations, even between strangers, can take place smoothly with a minimum of interruptions (simultaneous talking) and very brief intervals between the ending of one person's speech and the beginning of the other's. The times between acts at this level of analysis are very brief—from less than a second (close to laboratory findings for reaction time) to a couple of seconds. Certainly this is one level where the action is. The many strong regularities in these analyses, regularities involving one act and another act just before or after it, are in marked contrast to the paucity of fruitful findings for the analyses of these same kinds of acts when summarized as scores for several minutes of interaction.

The study of acts at this level of analysis can contribute to the understanding of the most important phenomena in the personality domain, the interactions between persons. The use of discrete acts located in time as units of observation also occurs in other frameworks, for example, behavior theory, behavior modification, human ethology, pupillometrics. The critical feature of all these approaches is the objective observation and recording of concrete pieces of behavior with minimal or no inference and interpretation by observers. In these approaches, we can have the standardization of variables and observational methods that London seeks (Chap. 7).

But are these acts important and do they help us to understand personality? They are important insofar as they throw light on human interactions. A judgment about their significance must be suspended, however, until much more of the difficult, laborious effort they demand has been expended on them. The regularities reported above had to be searched for; they were not the result of simple empirical tests of speculations made in a couple of afternoons. It does seem likely that the study of acts will illuminate the actual moment-to-moment processes in interactions. Whether such research contributes to our understanding of personality is not clear. If the term *personality* refers to the perceptions that people have about other people, there may be only tenuous connections. If personality is taken to mean the common and individual characteristics of persons in their interactions, then the potential contribution is great. The potentiality seems particularly promising in contrast to our previous efforts in the personality field, where the theories have been drawn from experience and can, it has even been suggested (Carlson, 1975, p. 411), be tested against our experience.

SUMMARY

The domain of personality is large and heterogeneous. It has been construed in many diverse ways because the constructs have been based upon perceptions and interpretations of personal experience, rather than upon empirical findings derived from objective observations. A real science must have maximal explicit consensus on its phenomena, concepts, and modes of operation. Personality does not seem to be progressing toward such consensus.

Personality has been oriented toward cosmopolitan concepts applied to people globally, even though its data are more or less specific to particular conditions. Scientific work in the study of personality phenomena must be based on provincial observations identified in time and located in space. Instead, time is blurred in personality research, an observation at a particular moment being taken as holding for some unspecified lengthy period. There is also a blurring or ignoring of the considerable specificity in the interpretive observations from any one observer, with the cognitive processes taken as general, not personal. The place within which the observations occur is blurred, as if it does not matter, in spite of extensive evidence that it does.

Most personality research involves averaging or summarizing a number of attributive judgments in an effort to estimate an a priori concept which is taken to exist regardless of what the data show. The usual concerns for reliability and validity stem from this state of affairs. If we take each act of a person just as an act occurring at a particular time in a particular place, we do not need to consider generalizability theory, except for the degree of agreement or interchangeability of observers.

Our cosmopolitan concepts and our taking of observations as signs, not samples, satisfice. We accept them as adequate solutions even though they are far from ideal answers to the scientific questions we ask. Overlooking all the slippage and blurring, we have grown accustomed to being easily satisficed.

Instead of muddling along as we have been doing, we can recognize several personologies, each focused on a particular kind of problem or type of observation. We can study the attributions that people make about people. Within the latter class, we can study societal problems in which society determines the concepts, the issues, and the appropriate observers for the basic evaluative judgments. Alternatively, we can study how people cognize and attribute. More generally, we can determine how people process the information they receive, how they construe people and behavior, and so on, as Mischel has advocated. Finally, we can study acts as they occur in the sequence of other acts. Whichever personology investigators choose, they must make explicit decisions, identifying the kind of phenomena, the way they will observe them, and the degree of intersubjective consensus on observations and constructs that will satisfy them.

REFERENCES

Ashton, S. G., & Goldberg, L. R. In response to Jackson's challenge: The comparative validity of personality scales constructed by the external (empirical) strategy and scales developed intuitively by experts, novices, and laymen. *Journal of Research in Personality,* 1973, 7, 1-20.

Campbell, D. T., & Stanley, J. L. Experimental and quasi-experimental designs for research on teaching. In N. L. Gage (Ed.), *Handbook of research on teaching.* Chicago: Rand McNally, 1963. (Reprinted as *Experimental and quasi-experimental designs for research.* Chicago: Rand McNally, 1966.)

Carlson, R. Personality. *Annual Review of Psychology,* 1975, *26,* 393–411.

Cronbach, L. J. Response sets and test validity. *Educational and Psychological Measurement,* 1946, *6,* 475–494.

Cronbach, L. J. Further evidence on response sets and test design. *Educational and Psychological Measurement,* 1950, *10,* 3–31.

Cronbach, L. J., Gleser, G. C., Nanda, H., & Rajaratnam, M. *The dependability of behavioral measurements: Theory of generalizability for scores and profiles.* New York: Wiley, 1972.

Deese, J. *Psychology as science and art.* New York: Harcourt Brace Jovanovich, 1972.

Duncan, S., Jr. Some signals and rules for taking speaking turns in conversations. *Journal of Personality and Social Psychology,* 1972, *23,* 283–292.

Duncan, S., Jr. On the structure of speaker-auditor interaction during speaking turns. *Language in Society,* 1974, *2,* 161–180.

Duncan, S., Jr., & Fiske, D. W. *Face-to-face interactions: Research, methods, and theory.* Hillsdale, N.J.: Erlbaum, 1977.

Fiske, D. W. Some hypotheses concerning test adequacy. *Educational and Psychological Measurement,* 1966, *26,* 69–88.

Fiske, D. W. *Measuring the concepts of personality.* Chicago: Aldine, 1971.

Fiske, D. W. Can a personality construct be validated empirically? *Psychological Bulletin,* 1973, *80,* 89–92.

Fiske, D. W. The limits for the conventional science of personality. *Journal of Personality,* 1974, *42,* 1–11.

Fiske, D. W. Personologies, abstractions, and interactions. In D. Magnusson & N. Endler (Eds.), *Personality at the crossroads: Current issues in interactional psychology.* Hillsdale, N.J.: Erlbaum, 1977.

Fiske, D. W. *Strategies for personality research: The observation versus interpretation of behavior.* San Francisco: Jossey-Bass, 1978.

Guttman, L. Integration of test design and analysis. In *Proceedings of the 1969 Invitational Conference on Testing Problems.* Princeton, N.J.: Educational Testing Service, 1970.

Jackson, D. N. The relative validity of scales prepared by naive item writers and those based on empirical methods of personality scale construction. *Educational and Psychological Measurement,* 1975, *35,* 361–370.

Kelly, G. A. *The psychology of personal constructs.* New York: Norton, 1955.

Kuhn, T. S. *The structure of scientific revolutions.* Chicago: University of Chicago Press, 1962.

Kuncel, R. B. Response processes and relative location of subject and item. *Educational and Psychological Measurement,* 1973, *33,* 545–563.

Kuncel, R. B., & Fiske, D. W. Stability of response process and response. *Educational and Psychological Measurement*, 1974, *34*, 743–755.

Loevinger, J. Person and population as psychometric concepts. *Psychological Review*, 1965, *72*, 143–155.

Mandler, G., & Kessen, W. *The language of psychology*. New York: Wiley, 1959.

Masterman, M. The nature of a paradigm. In I. Lakatos & A. Musgrave (Eds.), *Criticism and the growth of knowledge*. Cambridge: Cambridge University Press, 1970.

Minor, M. J., & Fiske, D. W. Response processes during the description of others. *Educational and Psychological Measurement*, 1976, *36*, 829–833.

Mischel, W. *Personality and assessment*. New York: Wiley, 1968.

Mischel, W. Continuity and change in personality. *American Psychologist*, 1969, *24*, 1012–1018.

Mischel, W. Direct vs. indirect personality assessment: Evidence and implications. *Journal of Consulting and Clinical Psychology*, 1972, *38*, 319–324.

Mischel, W. Toward a cognitive social learning reconceptualization of personality. *Psychological Review*, 1973, *80*, 252–283.

Mischel, W. The interaction of person and situation. In D. Magnusson & N. Endler (Eds.), *Personality at the crossroads: Current issues in interactional psychology*. Hillsdale, N.J.: Erlbaum, 1977.

Rosenthal, R. *Experimenter effects in behavioral research*. New York: Appleton-Century-Crofts, 1966.

Rosenthal, R., & Rosnow, R. L. *Artifact in behavioral research*. New York: Academic Press, 1969.

Rosenthal, R., & Rosnow, R. L. *The volunteer subject*. New York: Wiley, 1975.

Simon, H. A. A behavioral model of rational choice. *Quarterly Journal of Economics*, 1955, *69*, 99–118.

Simon, H. A. Motivational and emotional controls of cognition. *Psychological Review*, 1967, *74*, 29–39.

3

A CORRECT TREATMENT OF TRAITS

NANCY HIRSCHBERG
University of Illinois at Chicago Circle

Personality traits are broad, enduring, relatively stable characteristics used to assess and explain behavior. Traits account for the fact that, under similar circumstances, one person behaves differently from another. It is part of the nature of traits that although they can change, they cannot change too much or too quickly. Their stability suggests that the behavior they describe will be relatively consistent from situation to similar situation; their breadth implies that similar behavior will be manifested in different situations.

In our normal dealings with people, we assess, describe, and

This paper was presented at the conference on Strategies of Personality Research, Chicago, August 29, 1975.

Portions of this paper were written at Frescal, France. There I profitted from the insights of Donald Davidson. Other portions of the paper were written with the help of the facilities of Bell Laboratories, Murray Hill, New Jersey.

predict behavior on the basis of traits. We explain people who rarely pick up a check at a restaurant by saying they are cheap. We describe as generous someone who gives large amounts of money to charity. We use acquisitiveness to explain excessive clothes buying and give sadism as a reason for wife beating. Indeed, it is hard to imagine how we could get along without the rich descriptive and explanatory resources provided by such trait words as agreeable, autocratic, benevolent, brutal, clumsy, courageous, covetous, domineering, ebullient, generous, gluttonous, jealous, Machiavellian, pedantic, skeptical, talkative, and vindictive.

But do personality traits have any place in a science of human behavior? Some recent wisdom says not. The two main lines of argument for the uselessness of personality traits in explaining behavior have been conceptual and empirical. Recent conceptual positions are that traits are only summaries of past behaviors (Mischel, 1968, 1973; Shweder, 1975, Note 1; Wiggins, Note 2) or are dispositional in character (Alston, 1970, 1975; Ryle, 1949; Brandt, 1970). According to either of these views, traits neither explain nor cause action. As Wiggins (Note 2) noted, traits are "lost causes" whose existence requires, rather than provides, a scientific explanation. This author contends that the summary view of traits is incomplete and the dispositional view, confused.

The empirical argument against traits has been that manifestations of traits rarely exhibit any transituational consistency; and when they do show some consistency, it can be accounted for in terms of a cognitive bias on the part of the person assessing the trait (Fiske, 1974, Chap. 2; Shweder, 1975, Note 1; D'Andrade, 1965). However, given certain theoretical considerations about traits, the lack of apparent transituational consistency can be explained.

CONCEPTUAL ARGUMENTS

The Summary View

The simplest view in the literature of how traits should be construed is the summary theory or view. As Brandt (1970) explained, "To ascribe a trait to a person is simply to affirm that a certain corresponding form of behavior has occurred in the person, frequently or relatively frequently in the past—perhaps with the 'implication' in some sense that the same frequency may be expected to continue" (p. 25). According to this view, a person is charismatic who frequently has demonstrated magnetic charm in the context of leadership; a person is courageous who frequently has stood fast in the face of danger. This view of traits would be false if there were examples of traits for which past manifestations need not have occurred, and it would be circular if there were no way to explain what constitutes having the trait other than to say that someone has the trait who does the sort of thing a person with that trait is apt to do.

Analysis of the Summary View

A major implication of the summary view is that traits can be correctly ascribed only if there have been past manifestations of those traits. This certainly seems true in regard to stylistic traits. Stylistic traits are those that do not imply a motive on the part of the agent, and many are defined in terms of a person's characteristic activity level—lethargic, low-keyed, vivacious, energetic, emotional. Invoking a stylistic trait does not generally lead to or suggest an explanation of the reason why a person performed a given action. To explain why someone broke a lamp, for example, by saying that the person was clumsy gives no hint of a reason because the action, as described was not intentional. But for nonstylistic traits that are invoked to characterize intentional actions—honest, domineering, thrifty, proud, jealous—past manifestations may or may not have occurred. A person might have failed to act simply because of lack of opportunity.

Brandt (1970) noted, "There is no evidence to suggest that it is self-contradictory to say that a person is T but has not behaved in a T-like way" (p. 26). Brave or courageous actions might never have occurred in the past simply because appropriate opportunities (e.g., danger) were not present. Benevolent actions may never have been performed because the appropriate conditions for behaving benevolently had not arisen. In Forster's

"Howard's End," for example, the wealthy and cultured Schlegel sisters suddenly found themselves confronted with an impecunious white-collar worker on whom they decided to bestow large sums of money—an idea that had never occurred to them before. But, when the opportunity presented itself, benevolence ostensibly was the trait they showed. Under the summary view, one would be led to conclude that the sisters had, after many years, suddenly become benevolent. However, traits are not states that materialize without warning. It would be more appropriate to say that the sisters had for the first time performed a benevolent action, not that they had suddenly, and for the first time, become benevolent. If we adopt the summary view of traits, we are faced with the dilemma of whether to say that one benevolent act does not make a person benevolent, or that a person becomes benevolent at the moment of performing a benevolent act.

Some traits are more likely to have been manifested in the past than others. Since we assume opportunities for sociability are frequent in our culture, we might not call a person sociable who had never performed a sociable act. Situations calling for courage, on the other hand, may be relatively infrequent. We would not be justified, therefore, in calling a person non-courageous who had never performed a courageous action, for we would not want to say a person suddenly became courageous when performing a courageous act for the first time. Thus, the summary theory of traits does not hold for traits that may be possessed without being manifested.

Nor does the summary view hold for traits that are like desires—jealous, amorous, adulterous. One can have desires without showing them (Alston, 1975). One can desire to be loved, but that desire might never be manifested in action because of conflicting desires, such as fear of rejection. Traits, such as jealously, that have the same properties as desires also have the property of not necessarily manifesting themselves in action. A jealous person might never perform a jealous action because fear of the consequences outweigh the desire to obtain revenge. Other traits that are closely related to desires, such as sadism, lechery, lust, greed, and covetousness, may seldom or never be manifested in action, even under appropriate conditions, because conflicting desires interfere.

The Dispositional View

Another theory of traits is the dispositional view, which characterizes traits in analogy with physical dispositions. Consider solubility in water: to say x is soluble in water is to say that if x were placed in water, x would dissolve. Or fragility: x is fragile provided x would break if it were dropped. Similarly, to say x is courageous is to say that in the face of danger x would stand fast. The dispositional form of the definition is that if x were in a certain kind of situation (S), x would emit a certain kind of response (R). Thus x is cooperative provided that if (reasonable) requests were made (S), x would comply (R). And x is contumacious if, and only if, in the face of authority (S), x would refuse to submit (R). A dispositional view of traits need not be deterministic; it can be modified to incorporate the fact that for any given S, an R would frequently, rather than always, occur. [A slightly more complex definition of traits is the mixed view (Alston, 1970, 1975) in which a trait is defined both as a summary of past behaviors and as a disposition.]

The dispositional view of traits adds at least two features to the summary view: (a) it mentions the conditions necessary for the occurrence of the manifestations of the traits, and (b) it entails predictions for the future. The difficulty with the dispositional view is that it has led some to conclude that trait names are nothing but the names of the actions they (conditionally) imply. Alston, who adopts the mixed view of traits, noted "desires 'really' explain actions, where traits do not" (1970, p. 87). He claimed, for example, that the analysis of politeness makes explicit what actions count as polite but cannot help explain why someone acted politely; that involves appeal to a desire.

According to the mixed view, to ascribe a trait T to a person is both to imply past manifestations of T-like actions and to imply that further T-like actions would occur under appropriate conditions. Because this view of traits defines them directly in terms of actions, it is assumed, by those holding this view, that traits are only surface constructs in a theoretical network and do not enter into interesting theoretical relations with deeper explanatory constructs like desires. I contend that, correctly understood, dispositional analyses of traits do not rule out the causal status of traits nor the possibility of traits entering into theoretical relationships with other constructs like beliefs and desires.

The Correct View

It is an illusion to suppose that dispositional analyses banish unobservables; they simply move them around. We say (truly enough) that if x *were* placed in water it would dissolve. Here the mystery gets hidden in the subjunctive, with its implication of a causal law. We could try saying that soluble x has a tendency to dissolve in water, or a capacity or potentiality to dissolve. But tendencies, capacities, or potentialities are no more observable than dispositions. Quine (1974) noted, "The disposition is a property in the object by virtue of which the circumstances cause the object to do (a). The 'by virtue' here is what defies explication" (p. 8).

Other obscurities often surface in dispositional analyses. For example, if courageous is defined as standing fast in the face of danger, what do we say about someone who runs away in the face of danger because more lives can be saved than by standing fast? If this possibility is to be admitted, as it should, then something must be added to the definition, such as "everything else being equal" or "provided the person could not be more courageous in some other way." Another example is cooperativeness, defined as complying with reasonable requests. But to understand this definition of cooperativeness, we would also have to understand "comply" and "reasonable." All this is not to argue that traits are not dispositions, but rather to show that dispositional analyses do not eliminate theoretical constructs in favor of well-defined observable or potential actions.

An alternative and more compelling analysis of dispositional definitions is to view the disposition as a causal property of the object. "Where the strong connection is wanted is between the disposition (solubility in water) and its realization (dissolving when in water). The body dissolves when in water by virtue of having the disposition. The 'virtual' connection is itself analogous to a causal one; 'by virtue of' is almost 'because of' " (Quine, 1974, p. 8). Quine continued:

> Each disposition, in my view, is a physical state or mechanism. A name for a specific disposition, e.g. solubility in water, deserves its place in the vocabulary of scientific theory as a name of a particular state or mechanism. In some cases, as in the case nowadays of solubility in water, we understand the physical details and are able to set them forth explicitly in terms of the arrangement and interaction of small bodies. Such a formulation, once achieved, can thenceforward even take the place of the old disposition term, or stand as its new definition.
>
> Where the general dispositional idiom has its use is as follows. By means of it, we can refer to a hypothetical state or mechanism that we do not yet understand, or to any of various such states or mechanisms, while merely specifying one of its characteristic effects, such as dissolution upon immersion in water. There are dispositions, such as intelligence, whose physical workings we can scarcely conjecture; the dispositional characterization is all we have to go on. Intelligence is the disposition to learn quickly, if I may oversimplify. By intelligence I still mean some attribute of the body, despite our ignorance concerning it; some durable physical state, perhaps a highly disjunctive one. (p. 10)

Seen in this light, dispositional definitions do not vitiate the potential explanatory power of the predicate being defined. Suppose someone asks, "Why did x stand fast in the face of danger?" The reply, "because x is courageous," is not circular because it rules out other possible causes of standing fast in the face of danger. Being struck with instant paralysis that prevented movement might be another cause of the same action, ruled out by the explanation. Something might dissolve in water and not be soluble (laser beams can make almost anything dissolve). Solubility explains why x dissolved in water because it rules out other possibilities such as dissolving because of a laser beam. In this example, the object has a characteristic (solubility) that other things do not have. It is this characteristic that causes the object to dissolve under certain conditions. To say something has a disposition does not merely say that it will always perform in a certain way under specified circumstances; it also says that the object has a causal makeup that accounts for the performance.

Conceived in this way, dispositions simply are the structures (often otherwise unknown and unobserved) that under specified conditions cause the specified performance. Thus, to say that an object has a certain disposition is to assign a lawlike regularity to it; to say of this pill that it is water soluble is to say it has a structure S such that whatever has S, and is placed in water, dissolves. If we also know of S that it persists except under known conditions, say, then S begins to take on the interest of an explanatory construct, however little else we know of its molecular or chemical construction.

Traits derive their explanatory power, then, by virtue of being embedded in a theoretical network. To give examples of how traits provide explanations is to give examples that vary in power and interest according to the specificity of the description of the action being explained: The more specific the description, the more the trait explains. Referring to courageousness as a reason for why x stood fast in the face of danger suggests a relatively modest explanation for the action (i.e., by ruling out other explanations). But, if courageousness helps explain why x ran from the police, reference to the trait becomes a more important explanation. Of course, more of the story might well be told: x believed that running from the police would cause the police to follow, in turn leaving innocent victims free from harassment; or x decided to be heroic in the situation; and so on. But even without these details, we know a lot if we know the agent acted in a given way because of being courageous. Knowing this much does not allow us to give a unique reconstruction of the agent's reasons and intentions, but it sets limits on the sort of detailed story that is possible.

Traits are like diseases that are recognized, at least to begin with, by their symptoms. Consider infectious mononucleosis. The original symptoms were a swollen spleen, high fever, and tiredness. Physicians discovered that these symptoms additionally involved an increase in white blood corpuscles. They assumed that, since an increase in white blood corpuscles is usually a reaction to some kind of infection, infectious mononucleosis caused the increase in white blood corpuscles. But, neither then nor now has the particular infection been identified. Should one say that mononucleosis is simply a shorthand summary of a particular set of symptoms? Or that it is the state (type of infection) that caused the symptoms? Construing infectious mononucleosis as a causal state leaves open the possibility of discovering the thing (virus, bacteria, etc.) that caused the symptoms. Suppose one asks why x is tired all the time. To give mononucleosis as the answer is to supply an explanation of a causal sort. As a cause, mononucleosis rules out alternative explanations for the symptom of tiredness. Viewing diseases as causal states allows (1) the possibility of supplying, locating, or identifying the causal agent; and (2) providing an explanation of observed symptoms.

Scientists generally acknowledge that certain genetic structures can cause many sorts of genetically determined diseases, such as phenylketenuria, color blindness, and hemophilia. Although today genes are viewed as the causes of certain diseases, historically they were considered unobservable constructs inferred from the outcome of a series of studies. Nevertheless, long before genes were physically identified, they were that (unobservable) that caused a certain set of symptoms.

Another way to approach this notion is to look at dispositional definitions, not as (inadequate) empirical substitutes for unobservables, but rather as promises to supply that causal agent that gives the reason for specific actions, symptoms, or manifestations. As Quine (1974) said, "I once expressed my view of dispositions by saying that a disposition term is a promissory note for an eventual description in mechanical terms" (p. 14). For physical characteristics (fragility, maleability, solubility), the dispositional definition hides a lawlike connection that, if explicated, would point to the cause, namely, some underlying microstructure that is responsible for the object's breaking, bending, or dissolving. The analogy to the microstructure for traits would be whatever it is that causes the person to perform in a certain way. There may be an underlying physical structure, ultimately discoverable, that would involve a direct physiological agent such as a biochemical or neurological basis of behavior.

One difference between physical and psychological dispositions is that, for psychological dispositions, the causal property may not be discoverable. Although I think that this is probably the case, an interesting example of a physical state causing a person to have a certain kind of personality is found in Herald's (1958) remark about Talleyrand, whose feet were extremely deformed and whose character was despicable: "Monsieur de Talleyrand's character has been determined by his feet" (p. 93). Another example from Herald is found in the passage: "She caught a chill and died of pneumonia, victim to an excess of patriotic zeal" (p. 101). However, even if one knew in advance that no physiological agent would be discovered that corresponded to a psychological disposition, this in no way precludes the predicate from being a causal state.

Hempel (1965) commented:

> It is often held that explanation in terms of motivating reasons, learned skills, personality traits, and the like, being dispositional in character, are for this reason noncausal. But this seems to me misleading. . . . For example, the attribution of venality to an agent will explain his having committed treason only in conjunction with suitable further assumptions, such as that he was offered a large bribe, which in virtue of his venal propensity led to the act in question. Here the offer of a bribe . . . may be said in everyday parlance, to have cause the explanandum event. Dispositional explanations of this kind, therefore, cannot be said to be noncausal. (p. 486)

Traits, Beliefs, and Desires

It is generally agreed that desires and beliefs (or networks of desires and beliefs) are causes of intentional action.[1] Traits have been viewed as being useful for the nonprofessional or the novelist but not for those who study theories of personality (Mischel, 1968, 1973). Mischel has urged, on empirical grounds, that cognitive and social learning variables be substituted for traits in the explanation of behavior. Alston's (1975) theoretical analysis of traits also places cognitive and social learning variables on the same deep theoretical level as beliefs and desires. Common traits, on the other hand, are viewed as less interesting theoretically than beliefs and desires. One argument is that traits are surface constructs, and reference to traits does not constitute

[1] An intentional action is one that, under some description, is performed for reasons, and reasons refer to an agent's network of beliefs and desires. A combination of a belief and a desire has been called a "primary" reason for intentional action. It has been argued elsewhere that a primary reason for an action is its cause (Davidson, 1963). Although it is generally conceded that beliefs and desires provide explanations of action (Brandt & Kim, 1963; Alston, 1975), the logical status of personality traits is less clear.

an important class of explanations of actions (Alston, 1970, 1975).

Mischel's proposed cognitive and social-learning variables, on inspection, may be classified as beliefs or desires or both. For example, Mischel argues for the importance of "perceiver encoding information" and "cognitive transformations" (e.g., selective attention). These would be belief variables. Similarly, "expectancies" about behavior outcomes and stimulus outcomes are belief variables, involving an individual's beliefs about behavioral consequences based on either personal behavior or the stimulus configuration. Plans (Miller, Galanter, & Pribram, 1960) and behavioral intentions (Dulany, 1968) also are belief variables. Mischel does not neglect what I am calling desires. He urges the importance of subjective stimulus values or utilities that reflect the degree to which individuals value various response outcomes. The way in which behavioral intentions are translated into behavior depends, not only on the beliefs the person has about certain states of affairs, but also on what the person wants to accomplish by behaving in a certain manner.

Many of the social learning and cognitive variables Mischel (1973; Chap. 1) proposed as alternatives to traits for the study of personality turn out to be desires and beliefs, the causal status of which is unquestioned. A more serious question is whether traits play an important role in the prediction and explanation of behavior. Although my analysis of traits as dispositions suggests that there is a causal mechanism involved, traits could still be excess baggage in a theoretical account of behavior. Beliefs and desires may be the only constructs necessary for a complete explanation of action. It must be demonstrated that traits supply information about the reasons for actions that differs from the information given by beliefs and desires; it must be shown that traits are not reducible to beliefs and desires.

As an example of the way in which traits differ from desires and beliefs, consider two answers to the question, Why did x eat the piece of cheese?

(a) x is greedy.
(b) x was hungry and believed that eating the cheese would assuage the hunger.

Both answers provide an explanation for action. Answer (a) gives a trait as an explanation for action and answer, (b) gives a desire and belief combination, but (a) gives information of a different sort than (b). Even if (b) were changed to: "x is chronically hungry and believes that eating cheese would satisfy that hunger," the answer would not imply that x is greedy. If we know that people are greedy, we know much more about them than that they desire to eat on a particular occasion. "Greed" means "acquisitive desire beyond reason."

Consider all of the eating actions in which a person engages. Each action could be explained on the basis of a different belief and desire combination. One could eat cheese because of hunger, because one adored cheese, because one was substituting eating for smoking, and so on. Greed tells us something different. It tells us the kind of desires a person is likely to have. A greedy person wants to eat and drink more than is reasonable. Traits differ from beliefs and desires in that they tend to last longer and be less specific. If you know persons who are covetous, you do not thereby know any particular desires they have but you do know that they are more apt to have desires of a certain sort (e.g., to possess things other people have) than do most people. And covetousness characterizes the type of desires these persons are likely to have whether they have those desires at any particular moment. In this example, the trait is broader than the desires that fall under it.

Some traits tell us about the types of beliefs a person is likely to have. Suspiciousness, for example, causes people to emphasize any clue suggesting that someone may take advantage of them. Paranoia is the tendency to have beliefs of persecution and of personal greatness. Patriotism implies positive beliefs about one's country. Persons who are opinionated hold obstinately to their beliefs. In the face of a conflict of desires, some traits tell us which desires will tend to be more heavily weighed in a decision to perform an action. Faced with a piece of cheese, greedy persons are more likely to eat it than nongreedy persons despite the fact that the former may be watching their weight. If we know people are weak-willed, we would predict that their desire not to smoke would be outweighed by their wanting a cigarette.

These examples illustrate the fact that many traits are

broader than any single set of belief and desire combinations. Someone can desire to change another person's attitude and believe that the way to do this is by giving that person a lot of information. The action that this belief and desire explains is that of, say, giving information at a party. One trait that explains such an action is "opinionated." But certainly an individual could impart information at a party to change someone's attitude without being opinionated. More applicable words might be "domineering" or "informative." If, however, the person "held obstinately to opinions" in a variety of situations, independent of any specific belief and desire combination, opinionated would be the more accurate term. And the trait, opinionated, gives an explanation for action different from any desire and belief combination.

That trait explanations are orthogonal to belief-desire explanations is perhaps best seen in cases in which an individual would not (or only quaintly) mention the trait as part of his or her reason for acting. Consider the trait of being inconsistent. Most people do not want to contradict themselves. Each time a person says something contradictory to previous utterances, a different belief and desire might be involved. Each of these belief-desire combinations are different from "inconsistent," which characterizes the whole pattern of utterances or behavior.

An interesting class of traits is that which involves direct causes of action. Consider two answers to the question: "Why did the woman yell shut up?"

(a) she was dyspeptic.
(b) she wanted quiet and believed that by saying shut up, everyone would become quiet.

The first answer, (a), is a trait explanation of an action, and (b) is a belief-desire explanation.

In this case the cause of action, or emotion, is known: the cause of dyspepsia is indigestion. Answer (a) explains the action by giving the information that the person was gloomy and irritable because of indigestion. Answer (b) gives the information that the person desired quiet and believed that she would get it by yelling shut up. Both answers explain the action but in quite different ways. Clearly, both explanations are causal.

Consider another case: "The man refused the invitation out of pride" (i.e., because he was proud). One could know this statement to be true without knowing the intention specific to the situation with which the agent acted, and hence without knowing the most directly relevant belief and desire. One might, of course, know a relevant belief and desire—perhaps the agent wanted to hurt the inviter and believed that refusing the invitation would accomplish that goal—without knowing that the agent's pride was involved. Since refusing is intentional, the fact that the agent refused an invitation provides the information that he intended to refuse it and that he had a reason to do so. Knowing, however, that pride caused the action tells more about the agent. Among other things it rules out refusal of the invitation because he was too busy, or because he was forgetful, or because he did not want to expose others to infection.

In this example, the trait points to the arena in which the beliefs and desires relevant to the action are to be found. But it would be a mistake to assume that someone who acts out of pride necessarily has self-esteem, reputation, or pride in mind at all. Some proud people may be unaware that they care about their self-esteem, so we might be unjustified in attributing a proud motive to them. They may intentionally perform acts that show their pride, although their reasons may not allude to whatever it is that pride requires, such as being overprotective about one's self-image. Thus, pride may help explain an action even though the agent is unaware of this fact.

People are more apt to use traits like pride, irresponsibility, inconsistency, and greed to characterize actions of others than themselves. Normally, "greed" is not given as an explanation of one's own actions. People might say of themselves that they married for money but not that they married because of acquisitiveness; they might covet another person's spouse but not state that they are covetous.

People are interested in deciding what to do, not in predicting their intentional behavior. We do not consciously consult conflicting desires and give a trait as an explanation of which desire won in the decision for action. Rather, we find that one desire will at some point outweigh other desires, and we act on the basis of the relative strength of the desires. Observers usually are not privy to the agent's desires, much less to their relative strengths; they must rely on different evidence. Since observers are rarely in on the weighing of considerations (beliefs and desires), they turn to knowledge of a larger pattern of past behavior, of how the weighing tended to turn out for the agent in previous similar cases.

Given the sort of evidence typically available to observers, there is a logical reason why they tend to explain behavior in terms of traits rather than beliefs and desires or intentions, which tend to be quoted by the agents themselves. Although this point is a conceptual one, there is empirical evidence that traits are used more by observers in explaining someone's actions, whereas the situations are used more by agents (Jones & Nisbett, 1971). The fact that we do not usually give traits as reasons for our own actions indirectly supports Golding's notion (Chap. 4) that there may be a conceptual reason for the lack of convergence between self-trait ratings and peer-trait ratings. We do not view the reasons for our actions in the same way others do. Agents and observers have different types of evidence at their disposal. Geis (Chap. 6) makes this point, but for different reasons. Despite the fact that traits and their measures leave a lot to be desired empirically (Mischel, 1968), they may be almost the only evidence on which the observer can base predictions.

In the present view, actions are explained by traits in a different, but equally important, way than they are by beliefs and desires. Actions are the main evidence for traits, just as they are the main evidence for beliefs and desires. The fact, however, that actions are evidence for traits does not show that traits are nothing but actions or tendencies to actions; traits cannot be reduced to actions any more than can beliefs and desires. Furthermore, it should cause no conceptual confusion that traits both explain and are evidenced by actions, for the same is true of beliefs and desires.

TOWARD A THEORY OF PERSONALITY

If the above analysis is correct, then at least three theoretical constructs are necessary to a theory of personality: traits, beliefs, and desires. As explained, even though beliefs and desires can perform part of the job of explaining actions, traits are an additional essential element for a theory of intentional action. Traits cause action directly, or they cause action indirectly by causing the agent's *selection* of particular beliefs and desires.

As illustrated by many of the examples, a single trait can involve a host of different belief and desire combinations, each of which explains a different action. What all the actions have in common is that they are explained by reference to the trait, because the selection of certain beliefs and desires over others is explained on the basis of a trait. For these cases, traits can be considered analogous to a two-valued function in which the first variable is a class of desires and the second a class of beliefs. Thus,

$$T = f(\text{class b, class d})$$

where T = trait
b = belief
d = desire

The function represents a complex interplay of theoretical constructs. The trait ranges over all sorts of beliefs and desires (provided each is relevant to the trait in question). On one occasion the trait picks up a belief about that occasion and an appropriate desire (which translates the belief into action); on another occasion the trait function may pick up a different belief (and the same, or different, desire), and so forth. It is anticipated that traits would be directly related to individual differences in psychological organizing principles (Golding, Chap. 4) or construction competencies (Mischel, Chap. 1). Traits would predict individual differences with respect to attention, selection, and interpretation of various aspects of the environment, that is, the different psychological structures we impose on the world.

Of course, the theoretical picture is far more complicated than I have presented it and must account for the various desire networks, belief networks, and their interactions. Distinctions should be made among various sorts of desires. Some, such as hunger, which are chronically repetitive and satisfiable are short-term desires; those that are not immediately reduced by gratification are long-term desires.

Similarly, different kinds of beliefs may be expected to

have different characteristics in terms of their chronicity. Some beliefs remain the same across a variety of situations. Traits, being relatively stable features of personality, are present as causal states even when no action is occurring or when no particular belief or desire is involved. This stability of traits does not necessarily imply that a person will manifest similar actions in different situations (assuming one can recognize similar actions or situations). Traits point to (or pick up, in a functional sense) those beliefs and desires causing the action. Thus, cheapness might explain the action of picking up the check (e.g., the guests believed they would have to pay less often if they paid the bill occasionally).

The knowledge that persons are sociable incorporates information about the kinds of desires and beliefs they are likely to have, independent of how they act in specific situations. Suppose we say that x and y are sociable if they enjoy being with other people. It does not follow that x and y are always or even often with other people; they may not have the chance (because they are in solitary confinement); or someone may have paid them to stay away from social gatherings. One person may be sociable and then start to shun parties because of increasingly poor hearing that causes embarassment; another may be sociable yet have only a few close friends (because of shyness); yet another may go to a party on one occasion but not on another, depending on the characteristics of the parties and the person's beliefs about those characteristics. In each of these examples, the action to be explained depends not only on the trait but on the particular belief and desire involved. No one of the three elements—desires, beliefs, and traits—would be expected to explain any single action; all three are involved in a theory of personality.

There are at least two major issues to which my remarks have not been directed. One involves the problem of specificity in personality as originally conceptualized by Mischel (1968; 1973). The problem is: What guarantee does one have that an analysis of behavior in terms of traits and beliefs and desires will not be as specific and idiosyncratic (for each individual) as alternative conceptualizations of personality have been? I am suggesting to those who conceptualize personality in terms of traits that they must add beliefs and desires; if they wish to explain and predict actions to those who conceptualize personality in terms of beliefs and desires, add traits. In either case, constructs are being added which bring more specificity to the theory.

My argument is that although traits, beliefs, and desires may be idiosyncratic for different individuals, they are not so idiosyncratic as to preclude generalizable laws. Somewhere between broadly generalized nomethetic laws (which apply to all individuals) and completely idiosyncratic predictions lies the possibility of theorizing about human behavior by taking types of people into account. That is, not all people will behave alike because their traits and beliefs and desires differ, but different subgroups of people will behave in similar ways and for similar reasons. Isolating various subgroups of people in terms of their similarity of traits and beliefs and desires allows for the possibility of generalizing to the same types of people. (For an explication of the notion of individual differences in terms of types or subgroups of people, both conceptually and methodologically, see Wiggins, 1973.) This point is expanded in the section on empirical considerations.

The second major issue to which a theory of personality must be addressed is that of an appropriate analysis of situations, similar in kind to the present analysis of traits. In my conceptualization of personality, beliefs play the major role in an assessment of situations. In fact, situations cannot be assessed independently of beliefs, as Golding perceptively noted. Similar to the notion of a typology of people would be the notion of a typology of situations (Magnusson & Ekehammar, 1973) in the context of the traits and desire and belief structures. Generalization would occur for types of people as well as types of situations in the realm of intentional action. A good example of the interplay between types of situations and people is found in Revelle's (1976) work on introverts and extroverts. Introverts do not differ greatly from extroverts under ordinary circimstances, but under stress (e.g., time pressure, drugs) the intellectual performance of introverts deteriorates, while the performance of extroverts improves.

EMPIRICAL CONSIDERATIONS

Transituational Generality

If the present conceptual analysis is generally correct, then the ultimate theoretical status of traits will not depend on empirical studies of the transituational generality of actions that purportedly correspond to traits. Some traits, like stylistic ones, will be expected to be transituationally general in terms of consistent action manifestations. The more interesting traits, however, which involve intentions and motives, will not necessarily exhibit generality in the sense of similar actions occurring in similar situations. Whether a specific action occurs depends on a complex interaction among traits, beliefs, desires, motives, goals, etc. No single psychological entity should be expected to carry all the weight in the prediction of action patterns. But neither would any single belief or desire, or even a network of beliefs and desires, be expected to exhibit transituational generality. As noted previously, some desires and beliefs are transitory, others are not. Thus, the correct answer to the question of whether actions caused by traits will be transituationally general is that it depends on the action, the trait, the belief, the desire and the situation, and the interaction among these entities.

Personality Measurement

The present analysis of traits suggests that more, rather than fewer, distinctions should be made among traits. In the simplest analysis, stylistic traits were distinguished from traits having an intentional character. This distinction was made by Allport (1937). Among intentional traits, those concerned with desires (jealous, acquisitive, greedy, covetous) were distinguished from those involving beliefs (skeptical, suspicious, credulous, paranoid). Some traits can be characterized in terms of the agent (patriotic, domineering, courageous), while other traits are best characterized by their effects on others (annoying, abusive). Some traits are probably more closely tied to actions than others simply because some desires and beliefs are more closely tied to actions than others. For example, wanting to ride on a roller coaster is a desire that explains an obvious set of actions, whereas wanting to be a doctor is a desire that is less clear regarding the kinds of actions to be explained. My notion that more distinctions should be made among traits departs radically from the idea that science will progress only if a few traits are selected for intensive study (London, Chap. 7).

Given the rather elegant manner in which an attempt has been made to measure beliefs and desires in decision theory, it is surprising that traits have been measured in fairly simplistic ways. The measurement models commonly used in personality research have been cumulative, usually based on self-report inventories. The assumption is that the more items one admits to, the more of the trait one has. As Loevinger (1957) noted, the measurement model should mirror the theoretical complexity of the trait; and the present analysis barely points to the probable complexity of many traits. The different sorts of traits only hinted at in this chapter probably would require different types of measurement models.

The many examples of traits to which agents might not admit (although they might be able to give a belief and desire in explaining their actions) suggest that it may be unreasonable to expect self-reports of traits to agree with peer reports, a point made by Golding and Geis. I would add that the agreement to be expected should be dictated by the theory of the trait. This is similar to Loevinger's notion of trait structuring (Loevinger, 1957); the theory of a given trait would set an upper limit on the correlation between the trait and nontest behaviors or between self- and peer report. (In my analysis of traits it would make more sense to obtain self-reports of beliefs and desires, saving traits for peer or observer ratings.)

One implication of the present analysis for personality measurement is that a concentrated effort should be put into the measurement of beliefs and desires. The measurement of beliefs must be involved if situations are to be assessed at all; and the measurement of desires is necessary to the ultimate prediction of intentional action. If one uses decision theory as an elegant model for the present analysis, the measurement sophistication found in decision theory should be mirrored by the measurement of beliefs and desires in personality research. It is assumed that the beliefs and desires involved in intentional actions relevant to personality could be measured in much the way they are in decision theory. In that theory, beliefs and desires (i.e., subjective probabilities and utilities) are inferred from a series of choices via a set of axioms. Mischel (1973) has argued that preferences might be important psychological characteristics for the study of personality. If preferences are conceptualized as the end products of desires and beliefs, preference measurement would be one of the immediately useful means of inferring desires. I suggest that variables new to personologists (beliefs and desires) be studied; and that the methodological sophistication of such measures should parallel that found in decision theory.

A Typological Model

An appropriate place to begin the study of the present conceptual scheme of traits is with a structural model in which at least five conceptual modes are involved: beliefs, desires, traits, persons, and situations. These modes can be thought of in psychological terminology as independent variables; the dependent variable would be some measure of intentional action. A typological measurement model that involves the classification of people, desires, beliefs, traits, and situations in terms of the dependent variable would reveal the amount of generalizability to be expected for each of the modes. And an ideal model would specify the interactions among the various classes of subjects, traits, situations, etc. A model such as Tucker's (1963, 1964, 1966, 1972) three-mode (or, in this case, *n*-mode) factor analytic model is one that I expect would have the greatest impact in personality measurement under the present theoretical view. Tucker's models all involve the detection and isolation of individual differences as a function of any number of data modes. In the present example, individual differences in action would be isolated as a function of situations, beliefs, desires, and traits.

Consider a simple example: Assume one had a variety of situations in which subjects were placed; further assume that the subject's beliefs about the situations could be assessed, ideally in terms of the way in which the subject behaved. These data generate a subject-by-belief-by-situation matrix, the dependent variable being the subject's behaviors. Tucker's models allow the determination and isolation of the various types of subjects (if there are such) who hold different beliefs about different situations. In the analysis, one can classify subjects who are similar (in terms of their beliefs about the situation), beliefs that are similar (in terms of the subjects and the situations), and situations that are similar. The beauty of the structural model is that it further allows the specification of the interaction among (in this example) types of subjects, types of beliefs, and types of situations. The prediction of behavior would depend on the extent and kind of the interactions.

The present conceptualization of traits would involve an extension of the Tucker model. Subjects would be classified as similar in terms of their traits, desires, and beliefs, given a number of situations; and the classification would be based on the dependent variables such as specific behavioral actions in the various situations. For any given data domain, the model would predict the amount of specificity (generalizability) to be expected.

Whether Tucker's models are used is not the major issue. What is important is that a model be used which mirrors the complexity of individual differences as dictated by the theory of traits. The use of structural models would not preclude the ultimate use of more dynamic models. This section only hints at the possibilities of various empirical directions that personality measurement should take, but those directions are a start on the long journey of theoretical confirmation.

REFERENCE NOTES

1. Shweder, R. A. *Illusory correlation and personality theory.* Paper presented at Mathematical Social Science Board Conference, Chapel Hill, North Carolina, 1974.
2. Wiggins, J. S. *In defense of traits.* Invited address at the Ninth Annual Symposium on Recent Developments in the Use of the MMPI, Los Angeles, 1974.

REFERENCES

Allport, G. W. *Personality: A psychological interpretation.* New York: Holt, 1937.

Alston, W. P. Toward a logical geography of personality: Traits and deeper lying personality characteristics. In M. K. Munitz (Ed.), *Mind, science, and history*. Albany, New York: State University of New York Press, 1970.

Alston, W. P. Traits, consistency, and conceptual alternatives for personality theory. *Journal for the Theory of Social Behavior,* 1975, *5,* 17-47.

Brandt, R. B. Traits of character: A conceptual analysis. *American Philosophical Quarterly,* 1970, *7,* 23-37.

Brandt, R. B., & Kim, J. Wants as explanations of actions. *Journal of Philosophy,* 1963, *60,* 425-435.

D'Andrade, R. G. Trait psychology and componential analysis, *American Anthropologist,* 1965, *67,* 215-228.

Davidson, D. Actions, reasons and causes. *The Journal of Philosophy,* 1963, *60,* 685-700.

Dulany, D. E. Awareness, rules, and propositional control: A confrontation with S-R behavior theory. In D. Horton & T. Dixon (Eds.), *Verbal behavior and S-R theory*. Englewood Cliffs, N.J.: Prentice-Hall, 1968, 340-387.

Fiske, D. W. The limits of the conventional science of personality. *Journal of Personality,* 1974, *42,* 1-11.

Hempel, C. G. *Aspects of scientific explanation and other essays in the philosophy of science.* New York: Free Press, 1965.

Herald, J. C. *Mistress to an age: A life of Madame de Stael.* New York: Bobbs-Merrill, 1958.

Jones, E. E., & Nisbett, R. E. *The actor and the observer: Divergent perceptions of the causes of behavior.* Morristown, N.J.: General Learning Press, 1971.

Loevinger, J. Objective tests as instruments of psychological theory. *Psychological Reports,* 1957, *3* (Monograph No. 9), 635-694.

Magnusson, D., & Ekehammar, B. An analysis of situational dimensions: A replication. *Multivariate Behavioral Research,* 1973, *8,* 331-339.

Miller, G., Galanter, E., & Pribram, K. *Plans and the structure of behavior.* New York: Holt, Rinehart, & Winston, 1960.

Mischel, W. *Personality and assessment.* New York: Wiley, 1968.

Mischel, W. Toward a cognitive social learning reconceptualization of personality. *Psychological Review,* 1973, *80,* 252-283.

Quine, W. V. *The roots of reference*. LaSalle, Ill.: Open Court, 1974.

Revelle, W. Introversion extroversion, time stress, and caffeine: Effect on verbal performance. *Science,* 1976, *192,* 149-150.

Ryle, G. *The concept of mind.* New York: Barnes & Noble, 1949.

Shweder, R. A. How relevant is an individual difference theory of personality? *Journal of Personality*, 1975, *43*, 455–484.

Tucker, L. R. Implications of factor analysis of three-way matrices for measurement of change. In C. W. Harris (Ed.), *Problems in measuring change*. Madison: University of Wisconsin Press, 1963.

Wiggins, N. Individual differences in human judgment: A multivariate approach. In L. Rappoport & D. Summer (Eds.), *Human judgment and social interaction*. New York: Holt, Rinehart, & Winston, 1973.

4

TOWARD A MORE ADEQUATE THEORY OF PERSONALITY: PSYCHOLOGICAL ORGANIZING PRINCIPLES

STEPHEN L. GOLDING
University of Illinois, Champaign-Urbana

In a paper presented at the Stockholm International Symposium on Interactional Psychology, Block (1977) reviewed the data on consistency within and convergence between S-data (self-report), O-data (observer report) and T-data ("objective" measurement) and concluded that:

> Within the domain of O- and S-personality data, given good methodology, indisputably strong relationships exist and . . .

An earlier version of this paper was presented at the Conference on Strategies for Personality Research at the University of Chicago, August 27-29, 1975.

Preparation of this paper was greatly facilitated by a research grant for "Assessment of Interpersonal Behavior," from the Grant Foundation to the author and D. R. Peterson.

> within the domain of T-personality data, the evidence for lawfulness and coherence is far more difficult to attain. . . . It is now incumbent upon us to consider *why this pattern of law and disorder exists and what strategies are likely to extend the realm of coherence so as to include as well the domain of T-data.* (italics added) (p. 68)

The issue of consistency among various types of measures of the "same" construct is not merely an empirical inconvenience to be solved by more ingenious, or perhaps reliable, measurement techniques. Hidden in the mostly empirical debate that surrounds this topic are some serious and fundamental questions that rarely are raised or openly debated. The ennui, aimlessness, or at times the paralyzing self-doubt that characterizes much of our current clinical-personality-social research has its roots, I believe, in our neglect of certain crucial theoretical issues and our preoccupation with the meaningfulness of rather naively conceptualized data (see Golding, 1975, 1977a, 1977b; Golding & Knudson, 1975).

One such issue has to do with our neglect of the epistemological status of the phenomena that are discovered, evaluated, and constrained by our current methodological procedures. To put the matter more concretely, I want to examine whether phenomena having by definition both behavioral (objective) and experiential (subjective) components can be investigated by methods that confuse or ignore important epistemological differences between these components. While some aspects of this issue relate to the empirical consistency of the data that we collect, the most fundamental concern is with the nature of empiricism in modern psychological research. In order to make the sequence of arguments more coherent, I would like to outline the thrust of my thesis.

1. Most critical appraisals of trait psychology are based upon empirical evidence of highly variable quality that points to the instability, inconsistency, and stimulus-bound nature of behavior. Such empirical findings are used to demonstrate the falsity of the basic nomological assumptions supposedly entailed by trait theory.
2. Because trait constructs to which such data are directed are poorly articulated, a variety of interpretations are

possible. To heap further confusion upon already existing ambiguities, the interpretations of trait concepts are themselves sufficiently ambiguous so that the purported corroboration or noncorroboration of a given interpretation has little or no logical force. The definitional ambiguity also permits ideological and metaphysical "projection," clouding the already muddy logical and empirical arguments with personal convictions about human nature, ethics, and so forth.

3. The logical, empirical, and definitional ambiguities, in conjunction with an aversion for dealing with crucial philosophical issues (e.g. the mind-body problem) leads to the chaotic, diffuse pattern of research and theoretical argument that pervades most of the field of personality at the present time.
4. An examination of the epistemological status of most of the phenomena that fall within the domain of personality and social behavior leads one to a series of tentative conclusions that have profound implications for theory construction and empirical investigations in this area. More specifically, the following conclusions are implied by such an examination:
   a. The so-called objective-behavioral criteria against which we have tested most personality-social-clinical hypotheses are either questionably relevant or, more modestly, deserving of considerably less respect than they are typically afforded. Furthermore, the selection of these criteria is insufficiently guided by theoretical considerations and is frequently based upon an overly narrow interpretation of "intersubjectivity."
   b. Most constructs about personality-social-clinical phenomena entail psychological criteria that are inextricably bound to the psychological reality of the perceiver and hence are not easily reducible to objective-behavioral criteria. The "psychological reality contingent" nature of these data is problematic because the realities differ in important ways from person to person.
   c. On empirical as well as intuitive grounds a core set of

constructs, termed "psychological organizing principles," are proposed to make the analysis of typical phenomena in the clinical-personality-social domain more analytically and theoretically tractable. These organizing principles are assumed to have been acquired during the person's development and are seen as necessary for an adequate psychological analysis of any given phenomenon because they allow us to predict, explain, and understand the psychological reality of individuals on the basis of intersubjectively available data.

d. Future research and theory in the area will remain relatively ambiguous and chaotic when evaluated against contemporary criteria, unless the metatheoretical underpinnings of our current research and measurement methodologies are closely examined and revised to make them compatible with the nature of the phenomena to be explained (see also Fiske, Chap. 2; Hirschberg, Chap. 3).

DEFINITIONAL AMBIGUITIES

There seems to be little doubt that human behavior, at the so-called behaviorally objective level, is unstable, inconsistent, and stimulus bound. Block's (1977) excellent review of this "objective" data makes it clear, however, that the majority of studies upon which such conclusions are based are flawed by serious methodological and psychometric errors. Additionally, it is difficult to assume that such data, regardless of their quality, have any serious logical implications for a traitlike theory of human psychological organization. I contend that objective criteria, as they have usually been defined and assessed, are of questionable epistemological status and are less relevant than traditionally assumed.

In my work, I have become increasingly sensitive to the definitional ambiguities surrounding the term "trait." By a rough subjective count, over 90% of the *empirical* articles I have seen have used the term without definition or reference to a definition. In light of the fact that these articles deal with various nomological assumptions surrounding particular trait constructs (such as inconsistency, cross-method convergence, and the like), such an absence of definitional detail is disturbing, to say the least. On the other hand, *theoretical* articles that specifically address the trait-situation controversy do present definitions, but upon closer inspection these definitions can be shown to hide important theoretical, philosophical, and methodological problems and controversies.

In a recent theoretical statement, Mischel (1973) presented the following as the core assumptions involved in the traitlike constructs:

1. Personality dispositions or traits—the basic units of personality—are relatively stable, highly consistent attributes that exert widely *generalized* causal effects on behavior.
2. These dispositions pervasively influence behavior across many situations and lead to consistency.
3. These dispositions are not directly observed, but are inferred from behavioral signs (trait indicators).

He then referenced his own book (Mischel, 1968) as a source of summarized empirical arguments against these assumptions. Is this definitional attempt explicit enough, and of sufficient logical structure to permit an unambiguous interpretation of the corroborative (or noncorroborative) empirical evidence? I think not. Consider first the structure of the definition. Its basic form is, traits are attributes. But, what kinds of attributes are intended as definitional of a trait? "Trait" is often used in such a way as to make "habit" or "generalized habit" a close, but not perfect, synonym. Is this what is intended in Mischel's definition? One suspects that this is not the case, but the ambiguity remains. Historically, trait has also had biological and genetic connotations. Are we to assume that traits or attributes are of the same character as eye color or susceptibility to sickle-cell anemia? In short, just what is the elaborated network of theoretical assumptions and empirical predictions that surround traitlike constructs and distinguish them from other constructs? One does not know, and for that reason it is not clear what bearing the empirical evidence has on the (unarticulated) construct (see also Wiggins, 1974).

This concern may seem like philosophical quibbling, but as Fiske and Hirschberg also imply (Chap. 3; Chap. 4) it is not. Personality theory and research cannot progress until investigators agree upon which phenomena require explanation. Obviously, not all behavioral or experiential attributes are logically equivalent candidates for traits. But, if the lines of demarcation are not drawn explicitly, we have no way to evaluate a given bit of empirical data, for we do not know if it is logically related to the theoretical issue at hand. Thus, for example, Mischel's demonstration of nonconvergence between multiple measures of attitudes toward authority (1968, pp. 21-23) or dependency (1968, pp. 27-28) *presupposes* the logical equivalence of the phenomena subsumed under each construct, but this presupposition is questionable (Block, 1977; Golding, 1977a). To quote from a previous paper (Golding, 1977a), "the degree of cross-method convergence . . . expected is itself a nomological assumption embedded in the theoretical particulars of a given construct" (p. 95). Without specification of those theoretical particulars, the existing empirical data speak weakly, at best, to the issues at hand.

The qualifiers "relatively stable," "highly consistent," and "exerts widely generalized causal effects" turn out to be equally ambiguous. Consider the phrase "highly consistent." By examining the empirical work cited, we see that highly consistent means cross-method convergence and large omega-squared ratios for persons in a persons-by-situation data matrix. In previous papers (Golding, 1975, 1977a, 1977b) I have tried to point out that such interpretations of consistency are of dubious value. Cross-method convergence, as it is usually defined, turns out to be an unwarranted and unnecessary expectation for most psychological constructs in the clinical-personality-social domain, and omega-squared ratios have little theoretical or empirical bearing on the consistency issue. Furthermore, the typical correlation coefficients reported to assess consistency (correlations between traits or performance measures across persons) are often inappropriate. In the typical study, some putative trait measure, assessed at time one, is correlated with its supposed behavioral referent at time two. Not only do investigators uniformly fail to take the attenuating effects of unreliability of *both* measures into account (Block, 1964), but more important, the form of the correlation itself is misleading. Most personality trait constructs entail a prediction of consistency within the individual unit of analysis, the person; and hence correlation coefficients aimed at the consistency issue should assess covariation between measures across time within the individual, rather than covariation between measures across individuals with time confounded. The two values will rarely be the same (Lykken, 1971; Norman, 1967).

The phrase, "exerts widely generalized causal effects on behavior," is also quite troublesome. I share Mischel's intellectual discomfort with the implicit assumption of many trait theorists that widely ranging patterns of behavior can be reduced to statements such as, "This is predictable because of x's anal-compulsive character structure," especially when the theorist relies on selective postdiction and is unable to demonstrate the reliability, much less the validity, of such sweeping clinical judgments. However, Mischel would be far better off attacking the logical incompleteness of most trait constructs, instead of basing his refutation on the implicit assumption that the theoretical networks surrounding most trait constructs are rich enough to allow for empirical refutation. They generally are not. Mischel's empirical evidence on this point falls far short of its mark, either because the trait theorist can weasel out of the implications of the data by claiming not to have predicted the phenomenon, or because the prediction itself is so trivial or outlandish that its noncorroboration has little logical force (Block, 1977).

Other Ambiguities and Confounds

I have used some of Mischel's writing as an example, but the problem is not unique to his work. Indeed, it seems to me that most work in this field, including my own to date, has ignored the definitional problems surrounding the trait construct. Even Allport's (1937, 1966) attempts to define the construct of trait seem to me to be incomplete. For example, while large sections of his 1937 text are devoted to the role of learning in the acquisition of traits, references to the genetic component of traits creep in and sometimes assume a figure to ground relationship. But then, how are we to understand traits? Allport claims they are learned, but they are also "always a fusion of habits and endowment rather than a colligation or chain of habits alone" (Allport, 1937, p. 292). I have no objection to a model that includes genetic factors, environmental pressures, and learning history (much like Meehl's notions on schizophrenia), but the model needs to be clear in its specification. Further complications arise when use is made of traits as dispositional concepts. Most of us now realize that the earlier behavioristic-positivistic prohibition against dispositional concepts is unjustifiable, and that both the physical and social sciences can and must rely upon some degree of dispositional explanation (Averill, 1973; Suppe, 1974). However, it will not do to invoke a "traits are predispositions" kind of argument without specifying what kinds of psychological processes are implied by a particular dispositional concept (Wiggins, 1974). Because the "traits are dispositions" argument is left unspecified, Mischel can cite behavioral inconsistency as noncorroborating evidence, and defenders of traits can reply that consistency or inconsistency at the behavioral level is not an appropriate implication of the dispositional aspect of traits.

A final source of confusion has to do with metaphysical and ideological connotations that surround a trait construct. The heredity-environment controversy lingers in the nether reaches of many of our minds and persistently crops up in debates about traits. Because the very word, "trait," has biological and genetic connotations, trait theorists, rightly or wrongly, are assumed to believe that human nature is basically immutable, are seen as implicitly blaming the victim (Ryan, 1971), and so forth. I do not wish to deny that much of psychology, at both theoretical and applied levels, is affected by the social and political mores of our time. Many research programs, therapeutic techniques, and social interventions have definite ideological and ethical proscriptions embedded in them, and this state of affairs is perhaps inescapable. Nevertheless, many of these kinds of arguments about traits seem to me to be specious and simple-minded. We all must make our value systems explicit, but the question of the nature of psychological traits seems far too important to be buried under an avalanche of ethical polemics. Belief in individual differences no more implies a reactionary attitude than belief in strict environmentalism makes one a liberal. Such ethical and ideological concerns are legitimately a part of social science theory and practice, but they cannot be the sole grounds for scientific belief.

BEHAVIOR, EXPERIENCE, AND PSYCHOLOGICAL ORGANIZING PRINCIPLES

Most attempts at psychological theorizing in the clinical-personality-social area have failed to clear the empirical hurdle implied by the question, How validly does this theory predict behavior? This hurdle has assumed terrifying importance because of the societal demand on social science to prove its merit and because most psychologists subscribe to a philosophy of science that equates the explanatory power (= goodness = validity) of a theory with its predictive power. Such a philosophy of science is not only antiquated in many respects (Meehl, 1967, 1970; Scriven, 1962; Suppe, 1974), but also susceptible to misinterpretation and misuse when applied to phenomena and theories in the clinical-personality-social domain. That is, the equating of explanation with prediction stands on dubious philosophical ground, and the acceptance of such an equivalence has led us into a research design style that is fraught with difficulties. Of the many that could be enumerated, two are most relevant here.

Predictions sans Theory, sans Logic

Lykken (1968) and Meehl (1967), in extraordinarily forceful (but apparently unappreciated) articles, argued that large proportions of existing research, in spite of the statistical significance of the results, are absolutely equivocal in their meaning. This is so because most research studies (a) pay little or no attention to developing the theory from which the predictions are made, (b) fail to develop any nomological net (Cronbach & Meehl, 1955) connecting theoretical terms to each other and to observables (or potential observables), and (c) devote little attention to developing the logical and necessary connections between theory and prediction that are required. As a consequence, the empirical data bear little or no relation to the theory they supposedly corroborate. The data dangle in a vacuum. Since most psychologists view philosophical analyses as "damnable metaphysics," the requirement that empirical studies be based upon philosophical justification as well as methodological correctness may seem misguided, if not heretical. Nevertheless, as psychology goes "round and round in the widening gyre" in pursuit of empirical truth, the requirement becomes all the more necessary.

To bring this rather abstract point down to concrete reality, consider the following, entirely too typical example. In several recent papers, Mischel (1977) cited work by D'Andrade (1974) and Shweder (1975) to the effect that perceived behavioral covariance structures (implicit personality theories) do not mirror the "real" covariance structures. The data *appear* to support this conclusion–the intercorrelation matrix obtained between behavior ratings averaged over group participants after hours of interaction does not closely resemble the intercorrelation matrix obtained between actual behavior observations by nonparticipant observers but does resemble the connotative similarity matrix between behavior descriptions obtained from the participants. The claim made on the basis of data such as these is that rating methodologies in general, and peer ratings in particular, are extensively confounded by such implicit personality theories. Furthermore, since these implicit covariance structures are assumed to be shared, the additional implication is that the coherence between self-rating and peer-rating data is artifactual. These studies are subject to a variety of methodological and psychometric criticisms, but, more important in the present context, they are epistemologically naive. What has been shown is that the covariance structure produced by an observer (or averaged observer) differs from that produced by group participants. Since the observers are coding behaviors while the participants are rating traits, the implicit assumption of the authors is that behavior codings are epistemologically more sovereign or truer or closer to empirical reality; thus, trait-rating data are biased because they don't mirror empirical reality.

As psychologists trained in modern scientific psychology, we are, of course, biased towards accepting this type of argument. Mere mention of behavior as the basis of one's measurement methodology seems to be enough to convince most of us that an unbiased, empirical rendering of the object has been accomplished. One must understand, however, that a behavioral coding rendering of an object is but one of the family of possible renderings. That data based upon behavioral coding methodologies can be valuable is not an issue. What is at stake is whether such a method has any right to claim epistemological primacy. Behavioral data may be more or less meaningful than other data, depending upon the phenomenon under examination, the use to which the data are to be put, and the extent to which a behavioral rendering is epistemologically consistent with the nomological net surrounding the construct of interest (Golding, 1977a). In the case of the D'Andrade-Schweder type of data, what an individual is perceived as doing by participants is simply different than what he or she is observed as doing by a nonparticipant. It is foolish to present one data source as more fundamental, criterial, or truer.

Confusion between Behavior and Experience

When a psychologist develops a theory about a particular construct, let us say aggressiveness, one usually expects that the theory will in some manner predict aggressive behavior. What, however, is meant by the phrase "aggressive behavior"? As psychologists, we are prone to tack the word "behavior" onto almost every descriptor in our vocabulary (e.g., perceptual behavior, emotional behavior, verbal behavior). It is as if we were trying to solve a basic epistemological problem by fiat. This is so because the term "behavior," in its normal usage, implies that the referent has an objective, physical existence that is consensually verifiable. Furthermore, the use of the term usually implies that the existence of the referent is not dependent upon the psychological processes of the observer. While human observations may be necessary to count aggressive behaviors, it is implied that, in the ideal, the observers function as highly sophisticated, mechanical transducers of objective information from one form to another. Theoretically, it is assumed that a machine could be built to perform the same task.

I do not think that such an analysis is justifiable on empirical as well as philosophical grounds. While much of psychology has tried to model itself on the physical sciences, I believe that it does not aid our understanding of psychological phenomena to assume that they have the same ontological status as physical phenomena. While I cannot precisely specify the criteria of demarcation between the two (or more) kinds of phenomena—I do not pretend to have solved the mind-body problem—one crucial difference is that the perception of psychological phenomena, and indeed their very existence, is inextricably bound up in the psychological processes of both the observer and the observed. The referents for terms like "aggressive behavior," "dominating behavior," or "affiliative behavior" are quite different than the referents for more physicalistic phenomena such as level of autonomic arousal, perceptual threshold, and the like. At one time psychology was considered to be the science of human behavior *and* experience. But now "scientific psychology . . . having first lost its soul, later its consciousness, seems finally to lose its mind altogether" (Feigl, 1958, p. 370). Is it really conceivable that we can have a rigorous science of human psychology without confronting the behavior-experience (mind-body) problem?

Some psychologists, mostly of a behavioral orientation, have argued in the spirit of logical positivism that no theoretical terms should be allowed in scientific statements about psychology unless they are completely reducible, via operational definition and reduction sentences, to concrete observables and observing operations. In light of modern developments in logic and the philosophy of science (Suppe, 1974), such a position seems untenable not only for the social sciences but for the physical sciences as well. I do not think we can escape from the apparent fact that many of the psychological phenomena that are entailed by theories in the clinical-personality-social domain are constructs, both in the methodological sense implied by Cronbach and Meehl (1955) and in the epistemological sense, that is, to some degree constructed by the observer. Investigators in the area of social perception (Bruner, 1957; Shaver, 1975; Taguiri & Petrullo, 1958) have always emphasized the constructed nature of social reality but have not in general drawn out the implications of this thesis. *If the qualitative and quantitative aspects of social and personality phenomena are dependent upon the psychological construal processes of observers, then the notion of an objective, behavioral criterion begins to vanish, and we must confront the issue of the relationship between behavior and experience head on.* If speaking of aggressive behavior is to be legitimate, it is surely equally defensible to speak of the perceptual processes of observers that result in the verbal attribution of aggressiveness. The two ways of dealing with the phenomenon under study are neither equivalent nor mutually exclusive. As Vernon (1933) pointed out long ago, the existence of most clinical-personality-social phenomena resides neither in the individual emitting the behavior nor in the perceptual processes of the observer, but rather exists as a conjoining of the two. I believe that most, or all, of the phenomena in these domains of study must be understood along these perceptual-psychological lines. It is difficult to think of a case where any objective criterion, ontologically independent of the perceptual-psychological transformations of observers, exists. Psychological constructs, and the behavioral as well as experiential referents that they entail, seem to exist at equivalent epistemological levels. The notion that some levels of the data are truer or more real than others does not seem defensible. Psychological constructs inevitably entail psychological as well as physical criteria.

I am aware that this position raises some very delicate philosophical and methodological questions. Some might raise the question, "If you claim that psychological constructs are properly validated against psychological as well as behavioral criteria, how do we know that these putative entities are not just metaphysical illusions? After all, psychology split away from philosophy precisely because of discomfort with metaphysics and a belief that science could only be built on a framework of empirical, consensually verifiable events." A more philosophically inclined critic might ask, "If we accept your thesis, scientific inquiry into these phenomena would seem impossible. If the phenomena exist fundamentally at the level of psychological as opposed to physical reality, and if each individual's psychology, and hence reality, is different, don't you end up in an epistemological prison of solipsism?" These questions are among the most important ones that modern psychology must face. I believe that adequate answers are not yet fully possible, but a partial solution may be attempted by bringing into the argument the concept of what I prefer to call psychological organizing principles.

PSYCHOLOGICAL ORGANIZING PRINCIPLES AND PSYCHOLOGICAL REALITY

As is evident from my arguments so far, I view human beings as being extraordinarily active in the process of responding to and constructing the psychological realities upon which they operate. Indeed, I have argued elsewhere (Golding, 1975, 1977a, 1977b) that, for purposes of psychological analysis, situations, behaviors, and other such psychological events exist, fundamentally, as perceived. Assuming that there are important individual differences in the construction of psychological realities given the putatively same objective stimulus conditions, how is it possible to achieve any scientific study of phenomena in the clinical-personality-social domain? It is here that we must rely upon the notion of psychological organizing principles. If psychological experience, and hence psychological reality, can be shown to be lawfully organized within the person, and further, if such organizational principles can be assessed and related to various developmental, genetic, and experiential events, then we can be in a position to study psychological phenomena at an epistemological level consistent with the phenomena themselves. Psychological research has been predicated, thus far, on an overly restrictive interpretation of the intersubjectivity requirement for scientific data. Since the experiential component (one is even tempted to say the psychologically real component) of most psychological phenomena appears to be intractable from an intersubjective viewpoint, we have attempted, without great success, to reduce all that we study to consensually verifiable behaviors. I contend that the experiential component of psychological phenomena can be scientifically tractable if (a) the principle of intersubjectivity as a given is replaced by intersubjectivity in principle; (b) we allow (or accept) probabilistic relationships between objective and subjective events; and (c) we conceptualize the relationship between the consensually objective and the individually subjective as being lawfully organized within the person. This lawful organization of subjective event structure vis-à-vis objective event structure is what I term a psychological organizing principle. If psychological realities vis-à-vis the same objective social stimulus conditions differ interindividually, then the pursuit of scientifically justifiable explanations of psychological phenomena can occur only if we discover the "dictionary" that translates experience from one individual's psychological reality to that of another. The task is one of discovering the principles by which experience, especially in reference to interpersonal interactions, is organized.

William Powers, in *Behavior: The Control of Perception* (1973), presented a thesis quite similar to the one advanced here. He argued that an organism's behavioral patterns must be understood as internally organized (he used a cybernetic model), and that the crucial elements in human behavioral dynamics are a variety of hierarchically organized perceptual control systems. The essential theme of the book is that what we would call subjective reality or subjective-event structure emerges several steps removed from primary sense organs, is the result of considerable processing, and is under the control of cybernetically organized perceptual control systems. While some of the perceptual control systems may be genetically determined, as appears to be the case with many so-called lower organisms, it seems reasonable to assume that most are learned. Powers's ideas are congruent with many recent developments in cognitive psychology and with the essense of many clinical theoretic approaches, particularly those of George Kelly and Harry Stack Sullivan. I believe that the thesis can also be extended to the idea of psychological organizing principles and so encompass the organizations of more molar experiential structures. Stated most succinctly, I believe that individuals learn a variety of control programs whose operations produce the psychological reality of the individual. Like Powers, I believe that these control programs are fundamentally concerned with the processing and construing of perceptual data, but I also believe their operation is more widespread, being fundamentally concerned with the coordination of higher order semantic operations. Such a series of organizing principles is quite similar to the Sullivan concept of *self-dynamism*, but unlike Sullivan, I do not believe we know enough about the development of such a system and its modes of operation to assume that its reference signals are fundamentally concerned with the management of anxiety.

The suggestion that psychological experience is structured and organized in lawful ways has a long history in the literature of both psychology and philosophy; indeed, with the exception of certain rigid variants of behaviorism, it is difficult to think of a major metatheoretical position in psychology that does not in some fashion touch on the idea of lawful psychological experience. Of the varied antecedent positions upon which I could draw (if this were a historical review), I would point to the Sullivan concept of the self-dynamism (Sullivan, 1953). It is, in fact, not difficult to define self-dynamism as an integrative set of acquired strategies for the maintenance of optimal levels of positive physical and semantic feedback. The strategy of *selective inattention,* for example, involves a biased processing of incoming (interpersonally relevant) stimuli by means of operations on permitted semantic implications.

In spite of such similarities to Sullivanian theory (and others as well; e.g., Kelly, Piaget), it is unfortunately true that no well-articulated theoretical statement of experiential structure and processing, based upon corroborative data as well as insightful observation, is available. Only a shadowly outline of such a position is discernible. Perhaps an example of how such organizing principles might be discovered will help to clarify the argument thus far presented.

Consider the problem of units in observation research. Regardless of theoretical persuasion, researchers who attempt to code behavior sequences acknowledge that defining the unit to be coded is a major and fundamental problem. Typical solutions, such as time-based units or sentence transitions, are simply arbitrary. Surprisingly, little attention has been given to the idea of allowing participants in the interaction to engage in their own, habitual, segmentation strategies (see, however, Newtson, 1976, for work that is headed in that direction). The question of how long such units might be and whether meaningfully consistent and patterned individual differences in length might exist is somewhat interesting but basically trivial. What would not be trivial would be a demonstration of such individual differences in the content and inter- and intraindividual behavioral transitions that are selected for segmentation. I think we all have knowledge by experience of such differences, but to demonstrate them empirically would raise a far more theoretically important question: What attentional mechanisms are responsible for the control of such segmentation? (By no simple coincidence, this is precisely the sort of question of concern in cognitive psychology, although the stimuli used are of a far simpler, but increasingly semantic, nature.) We would, of course, expect that instructional set and other task variables, as well as culturally shared segmentation rules, would influence segmentation, but important individual differences should also emerge. Pursuit of the nature and the means of acquisition of these differences would constitute one strategy for discovery of psychological organizing principles. The discovery of such a set of attention-organizing principles would be valuable in solving a variety of seemingly intractable problems in current clinical-personality-social research. In addition to the units problem alluded to earlier, it would enable us to study impression formation, attribution processes, and other issues in social perception without resorting to the highly constraining (and possibly validity limiting) experimental procedure of prepackaged presentation of cues. We suspect that such experimental artifice biases our results because it does not allow subjects to extract information according to their habitual modes of doing so. This problem of just what a subject extracts from a particular objective stimulus field is related, in a rather obvious fashion, to the question of the relationship of behavior to experience and the organization of that experience.

The existence of such psychological organizing principles is, at the present time, a matter of speculation. While I cannot prove their existence or produce anything like a fully articulated set of nomological assumptions, axioms, and postulates, I am convinced that such a conceptualization will be a guiding force in future research. My faith in the heuristic value of this concept is based upon a number of factors that I can partially enumerate. I am convinced that at a purely epistemological level, psychology has been mistaken in attempting to reduce psychological phenomena to purely physical and objective behavioral criteria, or, at most, to see psychological events as mere epiphenomena. I cannot see how adequate explanation of most psychological phenomena can occur without dealing with the issue of the relationship between behavior and experience and coming to grips with the apparent fact of individually different psychological realities. Such individual differences can be demonstrated empirically (Golding, 1977b), but they are also experimentally apparent to anyone who deals clinically, empirically, or theoretically with interpersonal behavior. Without currently available empirical proof, the major leap of faith with respect to the concept of psychological organizing principles occurs with respect to the assumption of organization and the presumed locus of this organization of experience. One could assume that the psychological experience of an individual at any point in time and in any particular environmental context is completely idiosyncratic, having been specifically learned at the mercy of the vicissitudes of nearly random environmental contingencies. Such a view of human psychological experience makes little sense to me. Like Powers, Sullivan, and others, I believe it is far more reasonable to assume that the existence of all organisms, including human beings, is predicated on the assumption of organization. And I can see no reason for not assuming that if physical and biological systems exhibit such organization, then psychological systems equally can be assumed to be so organized, and it should be possible to discover the principles that govern this organization. Significant aspects of this organization may be genetically constrained, and to some appreciable extent the organization of experience within one individual may be interchangeable with another individual, as a function of powerful situational constraints. Nevertheless, my own conviction is that the most significant aspects of this organization of experience is acquired (within genetic constraints) and operates primarily from within the person.

This idea of psychological principles is crucial in our analyses of clinical-personality-social phenomena because it focuses on the neglected problem of psychological reality. If this thesis has any sense to it, we should be able to develop a truly psychological science instead of a discipline filled with mixed metaphors and confused epistemology. First and foremost, the idea of psychological organizing principles dictates that our data and our methods of analyses must be congruent with the nature of the phenomena that we study. For example, most personality researchers apparently have been convinced by Allen Edwards's argument that social desirability response set is a major determinant of item endorsement on most personality and attitude inventories. Edwards reported correlations above .90 between mean item-endorsement frequency and mean item social-desirability scale values calculated over most commonly used item sets. Few researchers seem aware of a penetrating and devastating article by Warren Norman (1967) that showed that, at the level of the individual, the correlation between the perceived social desirability of an item and the probability that the individual will endorse the item hovers around .30. Individual differences of this sort can be strong and pervasive, and our methods of data collection and analysis should allow them to emerge when they are present.

The hypothesized existence of psychological organizing principles, potentially different from one individual to another, is an important conceptual heuristic because it leads us into a position of always keeping basic epistomological issues clearly in mind. In the examples cited thus far, we would never have assumed so cavalierly that situations or an item's social desirability exist as objective or intersubjectively valid events independent of the psychological processes of the person. We would have proceeded with the question of individual differences in the psychological organization of experience weighing heavily on our minds. The concern that theories and methodologies be consistent with the phenomena under study (see also Golding, 1977a) has special importance when the domain of interest is interpersonal in nature. When the behavior–experience relationship goes across persons, the problem of perceptual–experiential transformations multiplies and even spirals (Laing, Phillipson, & Lee, 1966). Consider the phenomenon of a so-called Machiavellian interpersonal orientation. In order to examine this phenomenon, we must consider the psychological realities of both the actor and the recipients of his or her actions. On the actor's side of things, we would assume that calling a person Machiavellian would imply some important things about his or her organization of psychological experience. Most fundamentally, it would imply that this individual is likely to construe social situations in a manner distinctively different than the so-called average individual. Recent research (Golding, 1977b) supports this assumption and indicates that such individuals (a) exhibit a generalized tendency to attribute unfriendless, hostility, and dishonesty to others, (b) tend to place much more weight than average individuals on the perceived dominance–submission of an interpersonal act in arriving at social judgments, and (c) tend to overattribute hostility and submissiveness to the same interpersonal acts that the average other sees as less hostile and more dominant. This type of research represents a first step in the directions advocated in this chapter, implying that it is possible to assess the construal-style component of an individual's psychological organizing principles and hence to begin to predict and explain the psychological reality of such an individual. As Bem and Allen (1974) have pointed out, we cannot assume that an experimental subject categorizes stimuli in the same fashion as an experimenter. If individuals differ with respect to their psychological organizing principles, and hence their psychological reality, we can hardly expect a group of individuals to manifest consistent construals, much less consistent behavior, across a sample of situations seen by the experimenter as psychologically equivalent. In order to keep the epistemological status of our measured variables at equivalent levels, we cannot measure individual differences psychologically and situations physically, as is usually done in most person–situation investigations. We cannot even rely upon the consensual perception of situations. Most current studies of the influence of situations on human behavior treat situations as forces (psychological as well as physical) whose existence is fundamentally independent of persons, ignoring highly significant individual differences (Alden-Wiggins, 1975; Golding, 1975a). As I have argued, however, situational forces reside primarily within the individual. Therefore, studies must take these factors into account. That individuals behave rather inconsistently across situations (as usually defined) tells us precious little about the predictive or explanatory value of personological constructs, unless we know that the experimenter's stimulus equivalence classes are isomorphic with those of the subject.

On the observer's side of things, we must take into account the fact that Machiavellianism is an interpersonal construct and hence must be assessed by the recipients of the so-called Machiavellian behavior. It will not do to assume a priori that Machiavellian behavior can be objectively indexed by a certain sequence of moves in Prisoner's Dilemma or other such objective measures. It may be inappropriate even to index Machiavellianism by the behavioral ratings, no matter how specific or noninferential, made by uninvolved observers. These indices may turn out to be equivalent measures of Machiavellian behavior (it would be more appropriate to speak of Machiavellian experience-engendering behavior), but this needs to be demonstrated. The Machiavellianness of the behavior as perceived by individuals involved with the actor is crucial to the analysis. That the behavior of the interactors may be encoded differently as a function of one's perspective is not a problem; it is a legitimate part of the phenomenon to be studied (Golding, 1977a). As psychologists, I believe we should be concerned primarily with prediction and explanation of psychological events and only secondarily concerned with putative behavioral reality. Insofar as psychology touts itself as a behavioral science, this may seem a strange contention, but I do not believe that it is. Almost all behavioral criteria of current concern can, upon examination, be shown to be fundamentally psychological in nature and dependent upon the interlocking of the psychologically organized experience of interactors. Individuals are not deemed psychotic solely because of the particulars of their behavior, but because the experience that their behavior engenders in others is psychologically processed in such a way as to lead the recipient into certain courses of action. Similarly, dominance is not defined solely or even primarily by number of speech interruptions, but rather by the experience engendered in the receiver. The interlocking of behavior and experience is a natural aspect of most of the phenomena that we study, and our methods, constructs, and epistemology must be consistent with the nature of the phenomena to be explained.

The apparent fact of individual differences in psychological organizing principles and corresponding psychological realities does not make the pursuit of lawful, scientific explanations of psychological phenomena any easier, but it also does not preclude the existence of such explanations. While the disappearance of apparently epistemological rock-bottom criteria is disturbing at first, it is not scientifically devastating. With respect to criteria, we must give up simpleminded objectivity and acknowledge the legitimate source dependency of our data (Chap. 2). It does not follow that there is, for any particular phenomenon, a heuristically useful infinity of perceptions. Everyone's perceptions are likely to be different, but for various practical and theoretical purposes, there will also be useful similarities. For given kinds of phenomena, we need to know what kinds of variables bound the limits of generalization.

Individuals who have relatively similar social-learning histories for reasons of sex, race, age, or subcultural identification are likely to have relatively similar psychological organizing principles. It should then be possible to predict variations in the criterial status of various phenomena for such subpopulations. Furthermore, as the psychological organizing principles of actors become more extreme, relative to the norm for any given phenomenon, we would expect consensus among recipients of the actions to increase. That is, in spite of individual differences in the psychological organizing principles of recipients, we would expect increased consensus as the psychological organization of the actor, and hence his or her behavior in psychological context, becomes more deviant.

With respect to the psychological organizing principles themselves, the primary problem is the absence of a sophisticated measurement methodology. Since Watson, the mainstream of psychology has eschewed self-report data and, in general, any data relevant to the operation of psychological processes within the black box. Most psychologists have a deeply ingrained suspiciousness about any form of self-report data, and consequently we are naive with respect to assessment techniques in this area. Existing self-report techniques primarily sample content, and while the psychological-behavioral-attitudinal statements that subjects are willing to endorse may bear a relationship to their psychological organizing principles, the relationship is likely to be quite indirect and susceptible to the influence of a number of extraneous variables. Techniques such as Kelley's REP test, or variants thereof (Bannister & Mair, 1968), are valuable but psychometrically cumbersome. Laboratory procedures, such as multidimensional scaling and information-processing models, are closer to home but are difficult to use except with the most abstract and simple stimuli, such as trait descriptors. Techniques from cognitive psychology, particularly those designed to investigate the structure and function of semantic memory, may prove to be useful, but they are unproven and too seldom utilized with naturally complex (ecologically representative) stimuli.

If the approach to the study of personality, with its complicated epistemological problems, is to proceed along the lines of delineating psychological organizing principles, new methodologies are clearly needed. For example, while I am painfully aware of the many psychometric problems that surround interview data, I believe that guided, Sullivanian-like interviews can offer a great deal as assessment devices. Such innovations, which are psychometrically sounder, are occurring. A recently completed study of marital interactional style, in which the primary goal was the development of a technique for assessing multiperspective perceptions within marital dyads, illustrates this (Knudson, Sommers, & Golding, Note 1). Following ideas set forth by R. D. Laing and his associates (Laing et al., 1966), we had at first developed a self-report refinement of the Interpersonal Perception Method but discarded it as artifactual, contaminated by response style, and so forth. As an alternative, we relied upon an inquiry technique in which, following a role-played interaction, each dyad member was shown the videotaped interaction in couple-defined segments and was interviewed in such a way as to elicit the multiperspective data in relatively natural language. The inquirers (interviewers) were programmed to get verbal statements that were codable without much observer inference, but they did not shape or selectively bias the responses. Such data reflect a close-to-natural readout of time-dependent perceptions of self and other in interactional context and so are closer approximations to assessing the construal-style component of psychological organizing principles. More techniques of this sort are needed. In particular, we must develop additional ways for assessing the encoding and decoding of social information, the operation of selective attention and information storage and retrieval, and most problematically, the operation of the higher order control programs themselves.

Each of us is aware, to a greater or lesser extent, of the flow of our own consciousness. Certain thoughts and perceptions occur, and are followed by other thoughts, perceptions, memories, and symbolizations of our own intentions and those of others. I do not assume that the flow of such psychological events and processes occurs randomly. Rather, each of us has learned within certain possible genetic constraints particular programs that govern the organization of such experience. These programs are what I call psychological organizing principles, and I believe that the development of new assessment methodologies aimed at their discovery and delineation will be the major task of personality research in the next decade.

I think that the concept of psychological organizing principles will help to reorient our research strategies and may emerge as a more basic unit of psychological analysis and inquiry. Such a replacement is necessary, because current concepts are based upon a confused epistemology that fails to distinguish between psychological and physical reality and to take their interaction into account. I have argued that the basic phenomena in the clinical–personality–social domain cannot be reduced to so-called objectively observable, physical events (Vernon, 1933; Suppe, 1974). Constructs and methods that serve to explain and predict such phenomena must exist and be tested at levels consistent with these phenomena. I believe that much psychological data is amenable to scientific treatment, even though the mainstream of psychology to date has tried to avoid this issue by viewing so-called soft psychological data as admissable only if they converge with hard, behaviorally objective data. While each individual's psychological reality is different, I contend that we can escape from the ultimate metaphysics of solipsism because the organization of psychological experience that constitutes this individual reality is principled, that is, is systematic and lawful. Moreover, for practical purposes, generalization across realities within certain (to be discovered) empirical bounds is possible. Thus, the concept of psychological organizing principles allows us to study psychological events properly, without rendering them nearly meaningless by inappropriate reductionism or retreating into solipsism. Much of what has been said about psychological organizing principles rests upon inference from empirical facts (e.g. individually different styles of interpersonal construal and the perception of situations). Other aspects of the argument are based upon epistomological assumptions about the differences of psychological as opposed to objective reality. Still other facets of the argument are based upon sheer speculation (e.g. that psychological experience is organized and that such organization is fundamentally acquired via learning processes). Last, we assume that the system, once constructed, tends to maintain itself through selective attention, selective choice of situations in which to function, congruency maintaining perceptions, and the like.

My own personal and clinical experience tells me that such assumptions are reasonable, but I think that scientifically defensible proof is also possible. In order to construct and test such a theory, however, we must come to grips with the need for a methodology that allows us to measure psychological experience, processes, and their organization at epistemological levels consistent with the phenomena under study. To come full circle, I do not believe that so-called objective or T-data can be expected to converge fully with data that occur at different epistemological levels. The important task that lies before us is one of discovering the principles by which experience is organized, and with that information I believe we can develop an epistemologically consistent science of psychology.

REFERENCE NOTE

1. Knudson, R., Sommers, A., & Golding, S. *Interpersonal perceptions of married couples in conflictual and decision making interactions.* Unpublished manuscript, 1977, in preparation.

REFERENCES

Alden-Wiggins, L. *Psychiatric ward atmosphere and behavior change.* Unpublished doctoral dissertation, University of Illinois, 1975.

Allport, G. *Personality: A psychological interpretation.* New York: Holt, Rinehart, & Winston, 1937.

Allport, G. Traits revisited. *American Psychologist,* 1966, *21*, 1-10.

Alston, W. P. Traits, consistency and conceptual alternatives for personality theory. *Journal for the Theory of Social Behavior*, 1975, *5*, 17-48.

Averill, J. R. The dis-position of psychological dispositions. *Journal of Experimental Research in Personality*, 1973, *6*, 275-282.

Bannister, D., & Mair, J. M. *The evaluation of personal constructs.* London: Academic Press, 1968.

Bem, D., & Allen, A. On predicting some of the people some of the time: The search for cross-situational consistencies in behavior. *Psychological Review,* 1974, *81,* 506-520.

Block, J. Recognizing attenuation effects in the strategy of research. *Psychological Bulletin,* 1964, *62,* 214-216.

Block, J. Recognizing the coherence of personality. In D. Magnusson & N. Endler (Eds.), *Personality at the cross-roads: Current issues in interactional psychology.* Hillsdale, N.J.: Erlbaum, 1977, pp. 37-64.

Brandt, R. B. Traits of character: A conceptual analysis. *American Philosophical Quarterly,* 1970, *7,* 23-37.

Bruner, J. S. Going beyond the information given. In H. E. Gruber, K. R. Hammond, and R. Jesser (Eds.), *Contemporary approaches to cognition.* Cambridge, Mass,: Harvard University Press, 1957.

Christie, R., & Geis, F. *Studies in machiavellianism.* New York: Academic Press, 1970.

Cronbach, L. J., & Meehl, P. E. Construct validity in psychological tests. *Psychological Bulletin,* 1955, *52,* 281-304.

D'Andrade, R. Memory and the assessment of behavior. In H. Blalock (Ed.), *Measurement in the social sciences,* Chicago: Aldine, 1974.

Ekehammar, B. Interactionism in psychology from a historical perspective. *Psychological Bulletin,* 1974, *81,* 1026-1048.

Fiske, D. A source of data is not a measuring instrument. *Journal of Abnormal Psychology,* 1975, *84,* 20-23.

Golding, S. L. Flies in the ointment: Methodological problems in the analysis of percent of variance due to persons and situations. *Psychological Bulletin,* 1975, *82,* 278-288.

Golding, S. L. Method variance, inadequate constructs, or things that go bump in the night? *Multivariate Behavioral Research,* 1977, *12,* 89-98. (a)

Golding, S. L. Individual differences in the construal of interpersonal interactions. In D. Magnusson & N. Endler (Eds.), *Personality at the cross-roads: Current issues in interactional psychology.* Hillsdale, N.J.: Erlbaum, 1977, pp. 401-408.

Golding, S. L., & Knudson, R. Multivariable-multimethod convergence in the domain of interpersonal behavior. *Multivariate Behavioral Research,* 1975, *10,* 425-443.

Kelly, G. *The psychology of personal constructs.* New York: Norton, 1955.

Laing, R. D., Phillipson, H., & Lee, A. R. *Interpersonal perception.* New York: Springer, 1966.

Lykken, D. Multiple factor analysis and personality research. *Journal of Experimental Research in Personality,* 1971, *5,* 161-170.

Magnusson, D. The individual and the situation in personality research (Supplement Report No. 30). Department of Psychology, University of Stockholm, Sweden, 1975.

Magnusson, D., & Endler, N. Interactional psychology: Current issues and future prospects. In D. Magnusson & N. Endler (Eds.), *Personality at the cross-roads: Current issues in interactional psychology.* Hillsdale, N.J.: Erlbaum, 1977, pp. 3-36.

Meehl, P. E. Theory testing in psychology and physics. *Philosophy of Science,* 1967, *34,* 103-115.

Meehl, P. E. Some methodological reflections on the difficulties of psychoanalytic research. In M. Radner & S. Winokur (Eds.), *Analyses of theories and methods of physics and philosophy. Minnesota studies in the philosophy of science* (Vol. IV). Minneapolis: University of Minnesota Press, 1970.

Mischel, W. *Personality and assessment.* New York: Wiley, 1968.
Mischel, W. Toward a cognitive social learning reconceptualization of personality. *Psychological Review,* 1973, *80,* 252-283.
Mischel, W. The interaction of person and situation. In D. Magnusson & N. Endler (Eds.), *Personality at the cross-roads: Current issues in interactional psychology.* Hillsdale, N.J.: Erlbaum, 1977, pp. 333-352.
Moos, R. Assessment of the psychosocial environments of community oriented psychiatric treatment programs. *Journal of Abnormal Psychology,* 1972, *79,* 9-18.
Moos, R. Conceptualization of human environments. *American Psychologist,* 1973, *28,* 652-665.
Newtson, D. Foundations of attribution: The perception of ongoing behavior. In J. Harvey, W. Ickes, & R. Kidd (Eds.), *New Directions in attribution research.* Hillsdale, N.J.: Erlbaum, 1976, pp. 223-248.
Norman, W. 2800 personality trait descriptions: Normative operating characteristics for a university population. Ann Arbor: University of Michigan, Office of Research Administration, 1967. (a)
Norman, W. On estimating psychological relationships: Social desirability and self-report. *Psychological Bulletin,* 1967, *67,* 273-292. (b)
Powers, W. *Behavior: The control of perception.* Chicago: Aldine, 1973.
Raush, H. Paradox, levels and junctures in person-situation systems. In D. Magnusson & N. Endler (Eds.), *Personality at the cross-roads: Current issues in interactional psychology.* Hillsdale, N.J.: Erlbaum, 1977, pp. 287-304.
Ryan, W. *Blaming the victim.* New York: Vintage Press, 1971.
Scriven, M. Explanations, predictions, and laws. In H. Feigl & G. Maxwell (Eds.), *Minnesota studies in the philosophy of science* (vol. III). Minneapolis: University of Minnesota Press, 1962.
Shaver, K. G. *An introduction to attribution processes.* Cambridge, Mass.: Winthrop, 1975.
Shweder, R. How relevant is an individual difference theory of personality. *Journal of Personality,* 1975, *43,* 455-484.
Sullivan, H. *The interpersonal theory of psychiatry.* New York: Norton, 1953.
Suppe, F. The search for philosophic understanding of scientific theories. In F. Suppe (Ed.), *The structure of scientific theories.* Urbana: University of Illinois Press, 1974.
Taguiri, R., & Petrullo, L. *Person perception and interpersonal behavior.* Stanford, Calif.: Stanford University Press, 1958.
Vernon, P. The biosocial nature of the personality trait. *Psychological Review,* 1933, *38,* 533-548.
Wiggins, J. S. In defense of traits. Paper presented at the *Ninth Annual Symposium on the MMPI,* Los Angeles, 1974.

5

THE PERSON IN THE PERSON X SITUATION PARADIGM: REFLECTIONS ON THE (P)ERSON IN LEWIN'S B = f(P, E)

RICHARD CHRISTIE
Columbia University

My approach to research on personality has been determined in large part by my possibly idiosyncratic interpretation of Kurt Lewin's cryptic formula, $B = f(P, E)$. What could be intuitively simpler than saying that behavior is a function of a person's interaction with the environment? There are grounds for my reading interpretations that Lewin had not intended into this overarching summary. As Deutsch (1969) pointed out, "Unfortunately, Lewin used each of his crucial terms, environment, person, and behavior, in several different ways" (p. 423). Given a formula that can serve as a projective device, various interpretations are possible. This is especially true since the original formulation was made over 40 years ago, before Lewin left Germany for the last time and before he had been exposed extensively to psychology in the United States, where personality theory was conceptualized in quite different terms than in his *A Dynamic Theory of Personality* (1935).

My interpretation of the personality and environmental interactions was influenced by a deep interest in the social psychology of political behavior (broadly defined) and by the developments in social psychology and personality theory in the immediate post-World War II period. I did not then nor do I now consider myself as a personality theorist. Rather, my interest has been in those aspects of personality that can be treated as persisting individual difference variables that interact with situational variables to determine behavior in laboratory and especially in extralaboratory settings.

My interpretation of Lewin's use of *f*, or function, was that of a phenomenological integration of the self (P) and the perceived environment in the life space. Although such a conceptualization is provocative, it is methodologically amorphous. At the time Lewin promulgated his formula in the mid 1930s, experimental design was, by present standards, in a primitive state (see Solomon, 1949, for a survey). Graduate students in the postwar period, however, were being introduced to analysis of variance designs in which it was possible simultaneously to vary individual difference and situational variables and to evaluate the interaction statistically. For one newly exposed to Fisher and explanations of how to extrapolate the methodology of ANOVA from agricultural plots to experimental designs in social psychology, it took a while for the relevance of the research paradigm to sink in. Once it did, the answer was obvious. Here was an efficient way to vary simultaneously the P and E in Lewin's formula, if they could be quantified.

THE 1940s: A SPIRIT OF OPTIMISM

There were two dominant lines of research in personality at Berkeley in the late 1940s. One was represented by Donald MacKinnon who, I was convinced, had read every article and book ever published on personality theory and research, remembered it all and had the material neatly categorized and organized, subject to revisions. He was, at least to one graduate student, the Diderot of personality and measurement. At the time I was there, he was establishing what was to become the Institute of Personality Assessment and Research.

The other motif was represented by Else Frenkel-Brunswik and Nevitt Sanford, who had completed the work later to be reported in *The Authoritarian-Personality* (Adorno, Frenkel-Brunswik, Levinson, & Sanford, 1950). This research was particularly provocative to me because of its political implications. Right wing authoritarianism made self-evident sense to one from the boondocks where prejudice was the norm, but the grounding of the authors' conceptualization in psychoanalytic theory made me think about the problem in a new light. And, miracle of miracles, the *F* scale tapping the authoritarian syndrome was an easily scored paper-and-pencil test which could serve as an individual difference measure in the P X S interaction.

Lewin's definition of the environment was perhaps a bit too subjective for my experimental taste, since he tended to conceptualize in terms of an individual's inferred life space. Experimentally oriented psychologists since the days of Wundt have manipulated objective (and usually limited) aspects of subjects' environments, as did Lewin himself. One of the reasons that I went to Berkeley for graduate study in the late 1940s was Egon Brunswik's concern for the ecological validity of stimuli in the environment. What valid inferences could be made by an observer from perceptual cues in the environment? Further, in Brunswik's emphasis on representative design, the focus was on the probabilistic distribution of cues in naturalistic as well as laboratory settings. This was a much more complex approach than that of traditional laboratory experimentation and more objective than Lewin's phenomenological approach.

A different emphasis on environmental variables was provided by Robert Tryon, who was then commencing his studies of covariation of individual difference variables with the cluster analysis of demographic variables. Yet a different approach was the use of survey analysis as reported by David Krech in the U.S. Strategic Bombing surveys and in my working with Seymour M. Lipsett on a survey of labor mobility. All in all, there was exposure to a number of provocative ways of conceptualizing environmental variables that were alternatives to or subsumed in Lewin's more subjective approach.

The sense of euphoria and optimism about the future of psychology and the use of personality variables in research permeated the Berkeley *Zeitgeist* of the time. In retrospect it is easy to see why. Both Sanford and MacKinnon had taken their PhDs with Henry Murray, who had worked with an unusually able and enthusiastic group of graduate students and whose *Explorations in Personality* (1938) reflected the first major sophisticated attempt to systematically assess personality. The expansion of psychology departments in the immediate postwar period to include training programs in clinical psychology gave a stamp of academic respectability, if not legitimacy, to the study of psychodynamics. Even hard-core experimentalists among the graduate students had their copies of Fenichel (1945), and even if they didn't agree with the tenets of psychoanalysis, they at least knew enough about them to argue pro and con.

At Berkeley we were especially fortunate in having as the dominant intellectual force and major theoretician, Edward Chase Tolman, who eclectically borrowed from Kurt Lewin as well as from psychoanalysis in his elaborate doodles of the life space of man and rat. Along with the sense of excitement in the rapid development of major theories designed to encompass all of human behavior, there was a permissive tolerance of concepts and constructs from a variety of theoretical viewpoints.

THE 1970s: WHAT HAPPENED?

It is sobering to compare the expectations of 1949, when I left Berkeley, with the recent state of disillusionment with the effectiveness of the use of individual differences in personality and social psychological research (Mischel, 1968, 1969). Sarason, Smith, and Diener (1975) have published an analysis of journal articles, comparing the proportion of studies using Personality X Situation designs and found that they had increased from 5% of the studies in 1950 to 14% in 1960 to 25% in 1970. Their search was triggered by the comments by Bowers (1973) and Endler (1973), among others, who argued that the interaction term accounted for more of the variance than did the influence of situations or individual predispositions alone.

Sarason et al. went on to analyze the amount of variance

accounted for in research articles in 1971 and 1972 by personality, situation, and their interaction. They noted, "Our survey reveals surprisingly low percentages of variance accounted for by all classes of variables investigated: situational, personality, demographic, and interactions among these variables" (p. 203). The median percentage of variance accounted for by personality variables was about 3% (Table 2, p. 202), which would imply a median correlation of about .17 between individual difference measures and the criterion measure. In an earlier review which covered the literature prior to 1958 on the relationships between personality measures and performance in small groups, Mann (1959) concluded, "In no case is the median correlation between an aspect of personality covered here and performance higher than .25 and the most of the median correlations are closer to .15" (p. 266).

Exact comparisons between the Mann and Sarason et al. analyses are difficult to make for a variety of reasons. Editorial standards were lower in earlier days, the journal rejection rate was lower, designs became more complex over the time studied, and so on. Despite these and other confounding factors, it would seem reasonable to expect that if there were a marked improvement in the validity of whatever it is that personality scales measure, then there would be some evidence of an increase in their predictive power as far as behavior is concerned. Yet, overall, there is no convincing evidence that this has happened.

In many respects the argument about personality variables is similar to that made against the use of attitudinal measures as predictors of behavior. Wicker (1969) has argued that a survey of the relationship between such measures indicates little predictive power.

In a broad sense, the bright hopes of a quarter century ago have not been generally fulfilled. In a review of the publications from McKinnon's Institute for Personality Assessment and Research, Clark (1960) pointed out that only about 5% of the obtained correlations were significant at the .05 level, Hathway (1972) voiced rueful second thoughts about why the widely used Minnesota Multiphasic Inventory has not been more robust, and Sundberg (1977), in a summary of personality assessment, noted that projective techniques, which were so enthusiastically embraced in the postwar period, have been largely discredited as research devices.

In view of all this negative evidence, it is possibly foolhardy to suggest that a closer look be taken at what is commonly acclaimed to have been a major disaster area. My own impressions are that this has occurred in part because Lewin's formula $B = f(P, E)$ has not been honored in research as much as it has been in the abstract. Everyone has favorite studies that are almost never cited. One of mine was by Haythorn, Couch, Haefner, Langham, and Carter (1956), which fits the Lewin formula nicely. The focus (B) was on leadership behavior. Half of their four main experimental groups had high *F*-scale respondents as leaders, half had respondents low on the *F* scale as leaders. Under each leadership condition the three followers were high scorers in half the cases and low scorers in the other half. The point of interest in this 2 X 2 design, in which the two categories of leaders were similar or dissimilar to their followers, is that it yielded significant interaction effects as well as significant main effects. Further, these differences were predicted on the basis of the authoritarian-personality research.

One of the interesting problems is why this study essentially disappeared from (or rarely appeared in) references. It was an extremely well-designed study, analysed with sophistication, published in a leading journal, and the authors included some who were highly visible in social psychological circles. Yet, the only reference I remember seeing that mentioned the interaction effect they found was in a review by Gibb (1969) in a chapter on leadership for the second edition of *The Handbook of Social Psychology*.[1] My interpretation is that it, as some other studies fitting the interaction model, did not attract wide attention because increasingly personality research was becoming identified with clinical research and social psychology was becoming oriented toward highly controlled laboratory manipulations. Even those people who gave lip service to the interactionist model were more likely, if they were personality oriented, to be focusing on trait interrelations or comparing clinical samples on individual diagnostic measures, and these

[1] A few days after the conference, I met one of the authors (Launor Carter) and told him I had just cited the articles as one of my favorite studies. He was surprised that anyone remembered it. He had forgotten about it until I described it in some detail.

efforts were not seen as germane by social psychologists who were much more attuned to manipulatable situational variables.

A CLOSER LOOK AT RELEVANT PERSONALITY MEASURES

Detailed reviews such as those by Mann and by Sarason et al. are valuable in giving an overview of trends and progress or the lack of it. One of the disadvantages is that studies of highly varying quality and relevance tend to be lumped together. A sophisticated study such as the one by Haythorn et al. has the same weight in a summary table as any one of a much larger number of studies not as well conceived and executed. Without singling out less adequate studies, it may be useful to make some general comments about the relevance of many personality measures used for research purposes, the sorts of situations in which they are used, the fit between personality and environmental factors, and the behavior measured as a result of the interaction.

Personality Measures and Social Psychology

One of the difficulties faced in a discussion of personality measures is defining which of the thousands of existing tests of individual differences are personality measures and which are not. This depends very much on how personality is defined. Endler and Magnussen (1976) distinguished five different personality models: trait, psychodynamic, situationism, interactionism, and phenomenology. Most of the existing personality tests are based on trait or psychodynamic models that assume consistency of behavior across situations. The focus is upon the organization of personality or the interrelatedness of various traits. In exaggerated form, this might be described as an abbreviated Lewinian formula, $B = f(P)$. One of the problems this creates for social psychological research is that many of these measures were originally based on a priori theoretical considerations (the Allport-Vernon Scale of Values, 1960) or the ability to empirically differentiate between populations that varied along some criterion measure (the MMPI, 1951; California

Psychological Inventory, 1957). Quite frequently, personality scales were based on samples from populations of psychiatric patients or other deviants and placed an emphasis on the detection of social malfunctioning.

The crucial point, however, is that most of these scales were not designed to predict behavior in interpersonal situations. Although some of them might prove relevant to such analysis, they were not designed to do so. Yet, any perusal of studies, such as those summarized by Mann and Sarason et al., indicates the widespread use of such scales for the prediction of behavior, even though there is little reason to expect success.

There are other critical points. First, it is impossible to escape the impression that in many instances investigators have engaged in what might be called the reification of scale titles and have assumed that because a particular instrument has a trait name, it validly measures that trait. Second, the assumption is often made that if a scale is reliable (and possibly valid) in an original standardization sample, then it is equally appropriate for a sample gathered years later that differs drastically in demographic and presumably psychological characteristics. Third, many investigators do not examine the technical properties of scales to find if their interpretation might be affected by such factors as contamination with acquiescence response set or social desirability, or if the item format such as agree-disagree, forced choice, etc. affects the interpretation of test results.

Situations

The use of situations in social psychological research has varied tremendously. Some researchers prefer naturally occurring situations that are believed to represent a setting in which certain behavior is expected to occur (e.g., studying leadership in infantry squads or industrial work groups). Others prefer to abstract aspects of behavior from the real world and try to reproduce the essential parameters in face-to-face interaction situations in the laboratory. Still others abstract even further and eliminate the physical presence of other people by simulating cues as to the "others' " behaviors through interaction with programmed confederates who may not exist in reality.

Any or all of these may be valid for particular research purposes, in the hope it is possible to generalize from more restrictive conditions to those occurring in nature. The interpretive problem in comparing studies is the extent to which one would expect the different types of situations to be comparable in providing settings for the operation of personality variables. Is a carefully designed simulation a better setting for the elicitation of behavior associated with a personality variable than a natural situation in which the presumably relevant aspects are inextricably entangled with other environmental factors that the investigator has not taken into account?

The Personality X Environment Fit

In my opinion, the argument as to whether personality, situation, or interaction is the most crucial term is a pseudoproblem. At one extreme, at least in theory, an enterprising experimenter (who would not have to worry about informed consent) could totally control the environment and shape behavior to the extent that persons, whatever their initial scores on personality measures, would display similar reactions. At the other extreme, by carefully selecting individuals with abnormally extreme positions on personality dimensions, one could elicit behavior that would be consistent across a variety of situations with low demand characteristics.

Most interactions of interest to social psychologists fortunately fall between these two extremes. Sarason et al. pointed out what the maximization of interaction variance should be: "The more theoretically relevant a personality or demographic variable is to the situation to be manipulated and/or the behavior to be studied, the more variance will be accounted for by the Person X Situation interaction" (p. 203). The problem in interpreting published studies involving Person X Situation interactions is that it is often difficult to tell how carefully this problem is handled. It is evidently ignored in many studies; to the extent that it is taken into account, there is frequently not enough information to determine exactly what considerations are involved in its implementation in the experimental design.

Measures of Behavior

One of the issues in the problem of predicting behavior by attitude measures, as pointed out by Fishbein and Ajzen (1974), is that attitude scales have a number of items approaching various aspects of the basic construct, so that a reliable measure is possible. Yet, frequently, only a single measure of behavior is used in which the respondent either displays or does not display the behavior in question. They note that the reliability of the response is unknown and that it is impossible to get high correlations between attitudes and presumed relevant behavior unless a composite behavior score can be obtained from a sampling of behaviors.

A study by Weigel and Newman (1976) illustrates this point. They designed a 16-item scale to measure attitudes toward environmental concern (conservation and pollution), with an alpha coefficient of .88. They then obtained a series of novel, relevant, and independent behavioral measures. First, they asked respondents to sign a petition supporting environmental conservation. Six weeks later, confederates asked respondents to participate in picking up roadside litter. Of those who agreed to participate, they also found out which ones actually participated. Eight weeks later, other confederates asked respondents to participate in recycling trash. They obtained not only initial agreement to do so but also actual measures of whether the respondents participated over an eight-week period.

These behaviors were clearly relevant to the Person X Situation paradigm. Most relevant here is the relationship between the individual difference paper-and-pencil measure and subsequent behavior. Weigel and Newman (1976) found an average correlation of .29 between the 14 discrete dependent measures and the original attitude scale. A somewhat higher average correlation of .42 was found between the mean of the three different types of dependent variables (signing petitions, participating in litter pickup, and participating in the recycling drive). Using a composite index of all three types of activities, an overall correlation of .62 was found.

The same basic principle should be true of personality measures used as predictors of behavior. In many studies a single dichotomous criterion is used; in others, especially in assessment studies, a variety of behavioral measures based on actual responses, observations, and other indicators are used as dependent measures. It is rare, however, that a composite behavioral index is used as a single summary score and its reliability reported.

A Pernicious Suggestion

One of the interesting characteristics of the data summarized by Sarason et al. (1975) is the fact that the distribution of the amount of variance accounted for by personality, situation, and interaction terms is highly skewed. The mean percentage of the variance accounted for by all three is less than their respective standard deviations and is therefore much lower than the respective medians. Although this can be interpreted in a number of ways, one possibility is that the relatively few studies that account for most of the variance in the composite analysis might do so because they are better designed (e.g., use more relevant personality variables, have stronger situational manipulations, or have a better fit between personality and situational variables).

If this is true, then an examination of the deviant cases might be informative. What do these successful studies have in common that the majority of marginal ones lack? The present view is that it would increase our understanding of the use of personality variables in research if we examined the differences between cases of success and of failure to find positive results rather than to engage in dubious debate about whether personality variables are important.

A CASE STUDY OF CONDITIONS NECESSARY FOR PERSON × SITUATION INTERACTION

In a dissertation by Florence Geis (1964, 1970), a correlation of .71 was found between scores on a paper-and-pencil test of individual differences and winnings in a complex interpersonal game. The fact that a test taken several months prior to the game predicted half the variance was gratifying in several ways. First, it was the highest such correlation with which I was familiar at the time. But almost as gratifying was my memory of Geis's comment when she was a beginning graduate student: "Every one knows paper-and-pencil tests can't predict behavior."

It is, I think instructive to examine her research along the lines discussed in the previous section. (See Geis, Chap. 6, for further discussion of this research.)

The Personality Measure

Geis used as a selection device combined scores on Mach IV and Mach V. These are both 20-item forms of statements based largely on modifications of those initially enunciated by Machiavelli in *The Prince* (1950a) and *The Discourses* (1950b). The first is given in a Likert format, the second in a forced-choice format. The scales differ from most in that the initial theoretical model was an interactionist one, neither trait nor psychodynamically oriented. The starting point was an interest in interpersonal manipulation and a theoretical analysis of what characteristics one would need to successfully manipulate the behavior of another. Writings of power theorists, both ancient and modern, were examined to see the congruence with the model, and Machiavelli's were selected as most relevant.

The 20 items keyed for Machiavellianism in both scales were selected from an initial pool of 71 that had been administered to three pools of undergraduates in the Midwest, South, and East for purposes of item analysis. The 20 items were selected from the 50 that showed significant part–whole correlations in all three samples. One-half of those chosen were worded so that agreement with an item was scored as high on Machiavellianism; the other half were chosen from among those in which the wording was reversed. In general, the items selected were those which had the highest part–whole correlations, although an attempt was made to discard items which essentially were alternative ways of expressing the same concept.

The scale, dubbed Mach IV, in a Likert format, was not subject to acquiescence response bias since the items were counterbalanced. It was found, however, that in a variety of samples the total scores on Mach IV correlated about –.35 with Edwards's scale of social desirability among samples of college males and about –.75 among college females. In short, agreement with Machiavelli was socially undesirable. Mach V was designed using a format in which each of the 20 items keyed for Machiavellianism was placed in a triad in which there was (1) an item empirically uncorrelated with Mach but with similarly rated social desirability, and (2) a buffer item that was high in social desirability if the matched items were rated as low in social desirability. If the matched items were low, the buffer was high in social desirability. The respondent then indicated which one of the three items was most like and which was least like him or her.

To return to Geis's study, she used scales that had been designed to measure orientations toward interpersonal manipulation. Scale construction followed what were then currently accepted canons, and the scales were designed to eliminate error variance caused by acquiescence response set and social desirability. The sample of respondents used in the experiment did not differ in any major respect from the samples of college students on which the scales had been standardized (although the Columbia College students used in the study did have slightly higher Mach scores than those in the initial samples).

Respondents were selected on the basis of their position on scores on both scales: those who were in the 4th, or upper, quartile on both and those who were in the 4th on one and the 3rd on the other were considered highs; those in the lowest quartile on both or in the 1st on one and in the 2nd on the other were considered lows; and the middle group was composed of those scoring in the 2nd and 3rd quartiles on both tests.

Overall, Geis's sample was selected to meet reasonably the criterion of the individual difference variable that was conceptually relevant to the experiment, and the selection procedures were designed to select those who met relevant criteria.

The Experimental Situation

At the time Geis designed the study, we were in the early stages of research on the Machiavellianism variable and were interested in maximizing the differential outcome of people who scored at different points on the scale. In addition, we were interested in giving participants different degrees of power, under the assumption that high Machs (good interpersonal manipulators) would wield it more astutely than low Machs. We also predicted on theoretical grounds (in part suggested but not tested in previous research) that high Machs would be more adept in their manipulations if power relationships were ambiguous rather than clear-cut.

The solution Geis adopted was her own adaptation of a three-person bargaining-coalition game described by Vinacke and

Arkoff (1957). Essentially, this is a Parcheesi-type game in which each player has a marker that can be moved down a path according to specified rules. Each player has a set of power cards, designated as high, middle, or low power by a number on each card. Each player, in turn, tosses a pair of dice, then has the option of multiplying the highest die value by any power card in hand and moving the marker the appropriate number of points toward the finish. However, any two or all players may make or break coalitions at any time, combine power cards on a particular roll, and divide the final pot according to agreement. To win a game, a player must reach the finish, a single winning player gets 100 points for the game, the others nothing. However, the 100 points can be divided in any amount agreed upon among the players. (For a full account of this game, see Geis, 1970.)

The ambiguous condition involved the same use of power cards, but the cards were held in each player's closed hand so the others didn't know what they were. In the unambiguous condition, the cards were laid face up in front of each player.

This was a complex game to run, because each player, whether high, middle, or low Mach, played in a tournament of six games and rotated through the three power positions under conditions of ambiguity or unambiguity. Under each of the latter conditions, each participant played with six other people, each with different Mach scores.

Basically, individuals were thrust into a situation in which they were told winning was a combination of chance (dice tosses), objective resources (power cards), and the test of individual skill in decision making (coalition formation). They were not aware of their own or the other players' Mach scores and had no way of knowing how the triads were composed.

Personality × Environment Fit Geis attempted to test as adequately as possible a particular individual difference variable, Mach scores. She also attempted to design an experimental situation in which Machiavellian tendencies would be allowed an optimum opportunity to display themselves.

Measures of Behavior Here the single most crucial dependent variable was the total number of points won in six games, each played under different conditions. Since about $1\frac{1}{2}$ hours were needed to complete the six games, there was ample time to engage in interpersonal manipulations. Clearly, this presents a more adequate behavioral measure for an individual than does a single game in which the power positions and ambiguity do not vary and there is only one set of opponents.

Comments on the Geis Experiment The study is interpreted as one that rather convincingly shows that it is possible to predict relevant behavior from a paper-and-pencil measure. The correlation of .71 between total Mach scores and the number of points won in the tournament testifies to the fact that a measure specifically designed to tap a general individual difference can predict theoretically relevant behavior. This is true, at least, when the investigator is as skilled in theoretical conceptualization as Geis and has her ability to translate hypotheses into empirically tested experimental form.

LIMITS ON THE PERSON X ENVIRONMENT INTERACTION: THE CASE OF MACHIAVELLIANISM

One of the virtues of continuing research with a particular variable or an experimental paradigm is that, with the accumulation of experiences, one can begin appropriately to modify original formulations and to see the limitations as well as the adequacies of a particular approach. This was the case with my $1\frac{1}{2}$ decades of studying the concept of Machiavellianism.

Ironically, perhaps, the original interest in interpersonal manipulation was not thought of in terms of laboratory studies on construct validity. Shils (1954) criticized the authoritarian-personality research on many grounds, but the criticism that made the most intuitive sense was that individuals who were highly suspicious of others and projected their own aggressive impulses on them were highly unlikely to be successful controllers of the behavior of others in an organizational setting. Mann's review (1958) subsequently presented material that bolstered this viewpoint: "The California *F* scale, a measure of authoritarian trends within the personality, has been used 10 times in the prediction of leadership. In each case, high-*F*, or authoritarian, individuals were found to be rated lower on leadership than nonauthoritarian individuals" (p. 249). Both a sociological critique and small-group research independently supported the notion that authoritarianism, as measured by the *F* scale, is not related to the successful leadership of others. A further and more crucial point is that the formal occupancy of leadership roles does not necessarily mean that the formal leaders make more crucial decisions. The initial focus of my interest was on the gray eminences, power brokers, or what have you, who were making the crucial decisions.

The earlier investigations of concomitants of the Mach scales were much more sociological than psychological. Would people who occupied social roles that required the manipulation and control of others actually obtain higher scores? Would occupational or cultural groups that varied along a dimension of traditionalism–modernism differ in mean Mach scores? How did the scales relate to other socially relevant individual difference variables?

This scanning of the social landscape was generally supportive of some of the initial hypotheses about the prevalence and location of high and low Machs. The first two known experimental studies using Mach scales were done by Jones and Daugherty (1959) and Jones, Davis, and Gergen (1961). They reported results that were interesting but essentially of trivial consequence for my interests because the interactions were with simulated others. The study that fired my imagination was one by Exline, Thibaut, Hickey, and Gumpert (1970). In this study (done in 1960), individuals who had previously taken the Mach IV scale were first put into a situation in which an experimental confederate induced them to cheat. When the guilty participants subsequently were interrogated by an experimenter about the procedures they used to make such unusually high scores on an experimental test, the interrogator became increasingly amazed and dissatisfied. He finally accused each subject of cheating. Unknown to the subject, an observer behind the interrogator was keeping a record of how often the accused looked the interrogator in the eye while resisting the charge of cheating. The high-Mach subjects denied cheating longer and stared the interrogator in the eye to a greater extent than did the low Machs.

The interpersonal behavior of high Machs in bluffing it out longer and more blatantly when accused (rightfully) of cheating seemed a clear case of defensive interpersonal manipulation. We wondered what would happen if an experimental opportunity were presented for offensive (in both senses) manipulation. The "Machiavel" study (Geis, Christie, & Nelson, 1970) was designed to test the hypothesis that high Machs would engage in more manipulation when placed in a situation in which the demand characteristics induced manipulative behaviors. High scorers performed significantly more manipulations, devised more varieties of deceptive ploys, and in postexperimental questions said they enjoyed doing it more.

With these findings, we began a series of studies to explore emerging hypotheses about the nature of the manipulations performed by high Machs, including those in Geis's con game. Most of these studies confirmed the experimental hypotheses and suggested further expansions and amplifications. However, one early experiment showed no significant difference between high and low Machs, and this had a major effect on considerations of the Person X Situation paradigm.

The study that did not produce positive results was based on the Miss Rheingold contest. One of the questions that interested us in the process of determining how high Machs outmanuevered their more trusting peers was the extent to which they were better able to pick up subtle cues about the nature of the experimental situation. They approached the experimental situation more as if it were a game, asked more questions about what was permissible, and in general seemed to catch on more quickly to the demand characteristics of situations, although we found no correlations between Mach scores and measures of intellectual ability. To what extent was their success due to a greater interest and more adequate reading of cues in the environment?

We hypothesized that if high Machs were generally more adept at picking up social cues, they should learn faster in a situation in which the correct cues were very subtle. The stimuli chosen were pictures of contestants in an annual contest sponsored by a brewery. Every year six young women were chosen from a large number of applicants to be contestants; their pictures were displayed in the magazine sections of newspapers, on billboards, and on posters and were omnipresent from Labor Day to Christmas, during which time the public was invited to vote. According to the company representative in charge of the contest, over 20 million votes were cast annually (many of them repeats, of course) and this seemed a sufficiently large number to be relatively uninfluenced by the votes solicited by the contestants' friends. More crucially, the ballots were independently tallied (for legal reasons), and the winning contestant often obtained over 40% of the total vote. Somehow, the unknown voters were in agreement on which one of the six similarly dressed, coifed, and photographed young women was most deserving of reigning as Miss Rheingold for a year.

For the study, we (Christie & Boehm, 1970) obtained the color photographs of the six contestants for each of the 20 years in which a Miss Rheingold had been elected. The pictures of the six contestants for a given year were mounted on slides and used as experimental stimuli. We then found a sample of respondents that had never been exposed to the Miss Rheingold contest and projected the slides in chronological order in a learning experiment. Participants were asked to study a slide and identify the one contestant they believed to be the winner; then the slide was reshown and the winner identified. The process was repeated with each group of slides. Somewhat to our surprise and gratification, the two basic assumptions underlying the stimuli were met. Winning contestants were identified at better than a chance level even on the beginning trials, and there was a significant increase in correct identification over the trials. Interestingly enough, the cues that the participants said they used had nothing to do with which contestant actually won. (Winners did not differ on any mentioned characteristic such as hair color or length, smile, dimples, retroussé nose, etc., with one exception: those looking directly at the camera were more likely to be winners than those who had their heads tilted in either the horizontal or vertical plane.)

The cues were subtle, and the majority of participants were learning to identify winners. Yet the crucial hypothesis was not confirmed–high Machs were neither better nor worse at picking up the cues.

The failure of this experiment to produce the predicted results initially was puzzling. However, as results from other studies became available, a pattern began to emerge that held true whether the experiments were done under our supervision or were done elsewhere with different subject pools. Geis and I found that we could make fairly good guesses as to whether a given study would produce the predicted results by reading the experimental procedures carefully. The next problem was trying to determine inductively what underlay our guesses. Gradually we were able to clarify and formalize the reasons (see Christie & Geis, 1970, pp. 286–294).

In reviewing the results of 50 experimental manipulations, we arbitrarily used the .05 level as the cutoff point for whether high Machs "won" or not. By winning we meant that they behaved according to theoretical expectations by outconning fellow participants, winning more points in competitions in which chicanery was an aid, being less persuadable or more persuasive in attitude change studies, or otherwise behaving congruently with theoretical predictions (i.e., by displaying construct validity).

High Machs won in 25 of the studies and lost in 25. We classified the studies with respect to the presence or absence of three situational parameters:

1. Was the experimental interaction face-to-face? High Machs were more likely to win in situations involving the physical presence of the person with whom they were playing than if they were interacting with a simulated other or if there was no interaction.
2. Was there latitude for improvisation? This was believed to show that it mattered whether a participant could improvise the content or timing of his responses.
3. Did the experiment involve the arousal of irrelevant affect? This was interpreted to mean that there was something in the nature of the situation that aroused feelings which interfered with a coldly rational mode of behavior, such as arguing against something in which the participant believed strongly versus arguing against a neutral topic, lying or cheating to gain one's own ends when it had clear consequences for the well-being of self or others.

The Miss Rheingold study met none of the three criteria. Participants judged photographs of unknown women; so there was no interaction. They had to make one of six choices; so they had no latitude for improvisation (for instance, inventing reasons to convince someone else why Contestant C deserved to win). And it was a straightforward learning experiment in which there was no competition with others. There was no reason for participation except that it was a required task, and some might have been interested to see how accurate they were.

The con game, on the other hand, did involve face-to-face interaction with others. There was ample opportunity for improvisation in deciding with whom, when, and to what extent to make or accept coalitions or argue about them. Since all participants got caught up in a spirited competitive tournament in which it was almost impossible to win without doublecrossing someone else, a good deal of irrelevant as well as relevant affect was involved.

Many studies, of course, did not fall neatly into the extreme categories in which all three situational parameters were present. When Geis and I compared those studies in which none, one, two, or all three of the situational parameters were present, the trend was clear-cut, as shown in Figure 1. In none of the 11 cases in which no situational parameters were present did the high Machs win or behave as predicted; they won in only 5 of the 13 instances in which one parameter was found in 7 of the 12 in which two parameters were present, and in 13 of the 14 in which all three were present.

The present argument is based on this simple demonstration of the need to have relevant aspects of the situation present before an individual difference variable (manipulativeness) manifests its effects in behavior of interest. This may seem an elementary, and obvious point. Although I would have agreed with it in the abstract prior to doing an experiment using Machiavellianism scores as the individual difference variable, it was not until I had completed a number of experiments that the relevant situational variables for eliciting Machiavellian behavior became clear. Once uncovered, the results seemed obvious: manipulation was enhanced if there were someone present with whom to interact and greater rein were given to manipulative techniques (greater latitude for improvisation), and it would be

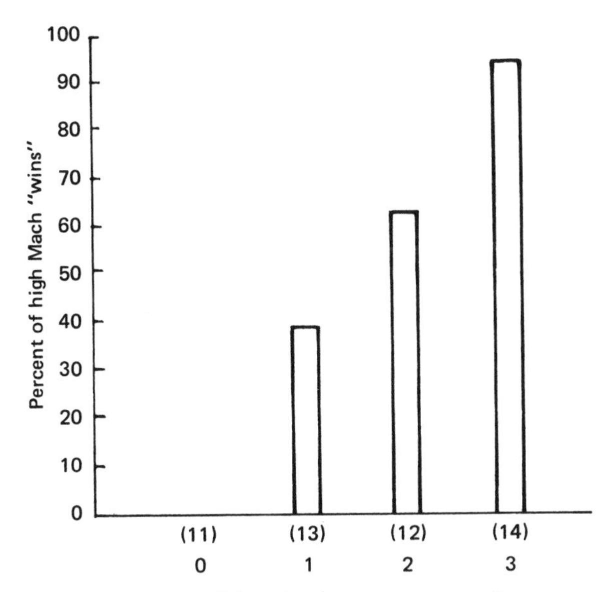

FIGURE 1 Relationship between the presence of situational parameters and successful performance of high Machiavellians.

displayed to a greater extent in situations that aroused feelings of ethical involvement. It was incredible that the findings had not been easily foreseen.

SOME GENERAL CONSIDERATIONS

My interpretation of Kurt Lewin's cryptic formula initially was shaped by my interpretations of his writing, by contact with professors who had been influenced by him, and most of all by trying to juggle simultaneously in a given piece of research variables dealing with behavior, the person, and the environment. The crucial point is that his formula, $B = f(P, E)$, is an interactive one with no single term predominant.

One's choice of a research area defines the sort of behavior in which one is most interested. In my case, a predeliction for the study of politically relevant behavior narrowed the scope of interest. But within such limits, to what extent does one focus upon person or individual difference variables or on those in the environment? Here there are two beginning strategies. One can focus upon an individual difference variable and ask which situational variables are best designed to elicit the theoretically relevant behavior, or one can examine the environmental or situational parameters and then determine what kinds of persons will best fit into them.

It is thus possible to start from either end of the person–situation continuum or from somewhere in the middle. Since it is easy to define the dependent variable (i.e., behavior), that is my preferred starting point. For the behavior that is of greatest interest to me, the environmental or situational requirements set the stage for what is possible or not possible in predicting that behavior.

What are the relevant dimensions of the environment? My argument is that they are not completely measured by the traditional tendency of Lewin and his students who rely upon manipulation checks, important as they are, to get a fix on the subject's or respondent's interpretation (or life space) of the investigator's manipulative chicanery. The environment is not a simple amalgamation of demographic background variables, since respondents may not be aware of what is "out there" as in survey research. My argument is that whether environmental variables are important depends upon the extent to which they engage or fail to engage relevant characteristics of the person in the situation.

Thus, we are thrown back in our never-closing circle to person variables. My experience suggests that, at least for political behavior, the most useful person variables for research are neither as highly specific as traits nor as amorphously global as psychodynamic concepts. Rather, they are quantitative measures with known reliability that capture that aspect of the individual's *Weltanschauung* relevant to his or her behavior in the environment of interest. For example, in jury selection for criminal cases, the variable of Machiavellianism does not seem to be relevant. An updated and modified version of the California *F* scale is more appropriate in the court environment where attitudes toward authority and law and order are central to the situation (Christie, 1976). In predicting the behavior of student protestors, both Mach- and *F*-scale scores are relevant but must be augmented by measures of New Left ideology (Gold, Christie, & Friedman, 1976) to construct a profile of scale scores that discriminates among protestors and their more complacent peers.

My conclusion is simple. A major reason for the failure to find many studies that indicate the predictive usefulness of personality measures in social psychological research is that investigators have neglected to take the Person X Situation paradigm seriously enough.

REFERENCES

Adorno, I. W., Frenkel-Brunswik, E., Levinson, D. J., & Sanford, R. N. *The authoritarian personality.* New York: Harper, 1950.

Allport, J. W., Vernon, P. E., & Lindzey, G. *A study of values.* Boston: Houghton-Mifflin, 1960.

Bowers, K. Situationism in psychology: An analysis and a critique. *Psychological Review,* 1973, *80,* 307–336.

Christie, R. Probability versus precedents: The social psychology of jury selection. In G. Bermant, C. Nameth, & N. Vidmar (Eds.), *Psychology and the law.* Lexington, Mass.: Lexington Press, 1976.

Christie, R., & Boehm, V. Machiavellians meet Miss Rheingold. In R. Christie & F. Geis (Eds.), *Studies in Machiavellianism.* New York: Academic Press, 1970.

Christie, R., & Geis, F. (Eds.). *Studies in Machiavellianism.* New York: Academic Press, 1970.

Clark, K. E. The mountain's mouse. *Contemporary Psychology,* 1960, *5,* 72–73.

Deutsch, M. Field theory in social psychology. In G. Lindzey & E. Aronson (Eds.), *The handbook of social psychology* (2nd ed.). Reading, Mass.: Addison-Wesley, 1969.

Edwards, A. L. *The social desirability variable in personality assessment and research.* New York: Dryden, 1957.

Endler, N. S. The person versus the situation—A pseudo issue? *Journal of Personality,* 1973, *41,* 287–303.

Endler, N. S., & Magnusson, D. (Eds.). *Interactional psychology and personality.* Washington: Hemisphere, 1975.

Exline, R. V., Thibaut, J., Hickey, C. B., & Gumpert, P. Visual interaction in relation to Machiavellianism and an unethical act. In R. Christie & F. Geis (Eds.), *Studies in Machiavellianism.* New York: Academic Press, 1970.

Fenichel, O. *The psychoanalytic theory of neurosis.* New York: Norton, 1945.

Fishbein, M., & Ajzen, I. Attitudes toward objects as predictors of single and multiple behavioral criteria. *Psychological Review,* 1974, *81,* 59–74.

Geis, F. *Machiavellianism and success in a three-person game.* Unpublished doctoral dissertation, Columbia University, 1964.

Geis, F. The con game. In R. Christie & F. Geis (Eds.), *Studies in Machiavellianism.* New York: Academic Press, 1970.

Geis, F., Christie, R., & Nelson, C. In search of the Machiavel. In R. Christie & F. Geis (Eds.), *Studies in Machiavellianism.* New York: Academic Press, 1970.

Gibb, C. A. Leadership. In G. Lindzey & E. Aronson (Eds.), *The handbook of social psychology* (2nd ed.). Reading, Mass.: Addison-Wesley, 1969.

Gold, A. R., Christie, R., & Friedman, L. H. *Fists and flowers: A social psychological interpretation of student dissent.* New York: Academic Press, 1976.

Gough, H. G. *California personality inventory manual.* Palo Alto, Calif.: Consulting Psychologists Press, 1957.

Hathway, S. Where have we gone wrong? The mystery of the missing progress. In J. N. Butcher (Ed.), *Objective personality assessment: Changing perspectives.* New York: Academic Press, 1972.

Hathway, S. R., & McKinley, J. C. *The Minnesota multiphasic personality inventory* (Rev. ed.). New York: Psychological Corp., 1951.

Haythorn, W., Haefner, D., Langham, P., Couch, A., & Carter, L. The effects of varying combinations of authoritarian and equalitarian leaders and followers. *Journal of Abnormal and Social Psychology,* 1956, *53,* 210–219.

Jones, E. E., & Daugherty, B. N. Political orientation and the perceptual effects of an anticipated interaction. *Journal of Abnormal and Social Psychology,* 1959, *59,* 340–349.

Jones, E. E., Davis, K. E., & Gergen, K. J. Role playing variations and their informational value for person perception. *Journal of Abnormal and Social Psychology,* 1961, *63,* 302–310.

Lewin, K. *A dynamic theory of personality.* New York: McGraw-Hill, 1935.

Lindzey, G., & Aronson, E. (Eds.). *The handbook of social psychology* (2nd ed.). Reading, Mass.: Addison-Wesley, 1969.

Machiavelli, N. *The Discourses.* New Haven, Conn.: Yale University Press, 1950. (a)

Machiavelli, N. *The Prince.* New York: Modern Library, 1950. (b)

Mann, R. D. A review of the relationships between personality and performance in small groups. *Psychological Bulletin,* 1959, *56,* 241–270.

Mischel, W. *Personality and assessment.* New York: Wiley, 1968.

Mischel, W. Continuity and change in personality. *American Psychologist,* 1969, *24,* 1012–1018.

Murray, H. A. *Explorations in personality.* New York: Oxford Press, 1938.

Sarason, I. G., Smith, R. E., & Diener, E. Personality research: Components of variance attributable to the person and the situation. *Journal of Personality and Social Psychology,* 1975, *32,* 199–204.

Shils, E. A. Authoritarianism: "Right" and "left." In R. Christie & M. Jahoda (Eds.), *Studies in the scope and method of the authoritarian personality*. Glencoe, Ill.: Free Press, 1954.

Solomon, R. L. An extension of control group design. *Psychological Bulletin,* 1949, *46,* 137-150.

Sundberg, N. *Assessment of persons.* Englewood Cliffs, N.J.: Prentice-Hall, 1977.

Vinacke, W. E., & Arkoff, A. An experimental study of coalitions in the triad. *American Sociological Review,* 1957, *22,* 406-414.

Weigel, R. H., & Newman, L. S. Increasing attitude-behavior correspondence by broadening the scope of the behavioral measure. *Journal of Personality and Social Psychology,* 1976, *33,* 793-802.

Wicker, A. W. Attitudes versus actions: The relationship of verbal and overt behavioral responses to attitude objects. *Journal of Social Issues,* 1969, *25,* 41-78.

6

THE PSYCHOLOGICAL SITUATION AND PERSONALITY TRAITS IN BEHAVIOR

FLORENCE L. GEIS
University of Delaware

The discovery of the situation in personality research may be something like the discovery of gravity in physics. We always knew it was there, but perhaps because it seemed so obvious, we took it for granted and often forgot it. Mischel's (1968) situationist critique of personality trait research is prompting a rethinking of the personality-situation relationship. The first point that must be acknowledged is the power of the situation. The whole history of research in psychology shows that the most consistent and predictable influence on human behavior is the situation in which it occurs. Although Sarason, Smith, and Diener (1975) argued that neither situational variables nor

I am indebted to Nancy Hirschberg, Donald Fiske, and Harvey London who read an earlier version of this chapter and provided helpful suggestions for improving it.

personality variables have accounted for much of the total variance in behavior, their survey of journal articles showed that significant situation effects have outnumbered personality effects by more than two to one.

But trait theorists need not despair. Indeed, their work is cut out for them. Obviously, the strongest, most dominant personality trait of human beings is "responsiveness to the situation." Obviously, also, there must be a range of individual differences in the strength or acuity of this trait.

On the other hand, it seems equally obvious that more traditional traits in the Allportian sense play some important role in human affairs. If personality traits did not exist, and behavior were *entirely* determined by the situation, it should make no difference at all to us who we sleep with—or marry, or ask to do us a favor. Persons would be completely interchangeable. Most of us act as if there were some consistent personal characteristics of people that lead us to prefer particular persons over equally available others in many interpersonal situations.

The problem, then, is to explain how situations determine behavior, given the existence of traits, and how traits influence behavior, given the force of the situation. The main point of this essay is that behavior is not a function of two separate forces, situations on the one hand and traits on the other; rather, behavior is a function of a single force, experience, which incorporates both situations and traits. This is the now-classic phenomenological position. Although situations and traits can be separated conceptually for purposes of analysis, I contend that behavior is a resultant of experience and that experience is an amalgam of person and situation. Experience is a construction of a person; it is the interpretation and meaning of a situation to a person. Although the meaning is easily misperceived as inherent in the external situation, it is in fact a construction of the interpreter. Idiosyncracies of the construction outcome that are relatively consistent within individuals but differ between individuals can be conceptualized as personality traits.

The principles by which persons construe situations to create experience were called "encoding strategies and personal constructs" by Mischel (1973), and are called "psychological organizing principles" by Golding (Chap. 4). Although Golding and I agree on this major point, we disagree about some of the conclusions implied in it. In this chapter the term "personality trait" is used in its broadest sense. Although distinctions can be made among traits, styles, attitudes, temperaments, character structures, abilities, defenses, and so on, I use the terms "trait" and "characteristic" as including all of these.

THE SITUATION AS A PSYCHOLOGICAL PHENOMENON

Most psychologists, both situationists and trait theorists, would probably agree that behavior is controlled by experience and that experience is a construction of a situation by a person. The problem is that taking the principle for granted, we forget it in practice. Then we proceed to build different psychologies, each on the basis of the selected constructs its separate proponents have made explicit. First considered in this chapter are some ways in which an explicit phenomenological approach would lead to different procedures, consequences, or conclusions from either the situationist or trait approaches.

What Is a Situation?

In our psychological journals, we often find the physical components of situations described in minute and exact detail. We are told the exact size of the room, the length and width of the table in centimeters, the capabilities and even the brand name of the slide projector, the physical characteristics of the task, and the sequence of events. However, the psychological characteristics of the situation are rarely described fully. Was the experimenter formal or casual with the subjects? Was the "group atmosphere" relaxed? Spontaneous? Bored? Defensive? What was the subject's experience? How did subjects construe the meaning of the situation? Typically, we assume that changes in the stimulus conditions that produced reliable differences in behavior did so because they were correlated with differences in subjects' experience. That assumption is probably correct, but it leaves ambiguous those very characteristics of the situation that were presumably crucial in determining behavior.

Where Is the Situation?

Although most psychologists speak and write as though the subject is in the situation, the explicit phenomenologist must argue that the situation is also in the subject. At least, the effective impact of the situation that "causes" the behavior is in the subject. Persons respond to the situation *as perceived.* Lewin (1936) saw behavior as a function of person and environment and insisted that people respond to their environment as experienced at the time. Murray (1938) made the same point with his distinction between "alpha press" (the objective situation) and "beta press" (the experienced situation). These early formulations are classic but insufficiently explicit. What does it mean to perceive an environment or a situation? It remained for the new look in perception in the 1940s and 1950s (e.g., Bruner, 1951; Postman, 1951) to demonstrate explicitly that perception is influenced by relevant hopes, fears, values, beliefs, and expectations. In short, this body of research demonstrated that perception is a construction of the perceiver.

More recently, Rosenthal (1974) has extended this principle. Not only is simple visual perception a construction of the perceiver, Rosenthal's data suggest that one person's psychological construction processes may influence another's behavior and the whole interpersonal situation. In the earlier perception research, children from poor families judged coins as larger than children from affluent families judged them; in Rosenthal's research, experimenters' expectations influenced their rats' performance, and teachers' expectations influenced their pupils' academic performance. The teachers' expectations also influenced their judgments of the pupils' personality traits and social competence.

If the effective impact of the situation depends upon an interpretation by a person, can we talk about a situation accurately as a fixed set of conditions, constant over subjects? A situation may have regularities but still be substantially different from one person to another. The evidence that a given situation (from the experimenter's point of view) in fact varies among subjects is the inevitable within-condition variance in our data.

Construction of Experience

The assertion that we construct our experience is platitudinous, a characteristic that facilitates its being taken for granted and forgotten. Let us consider three historical behavior patterns for which an explicit phenomenology would yield a different analysis from either situationist or trait approaches.

1. Some few hundred years ago our ancestors were burning witches at the stake.
2. More recently, well-bred ladies of the Victorian era allegedly fainted at the mention of legs or other parts of the human anatomy.
3. More recently still (Goldberg, 1968), subjects rated essays attributed to female authors as less persuasive and less intelligent than the identical essays attributed to male authors.

What were the causes of these behaviors? Let us review the point of view of the people involved, the naive situationist analysis, the naive trait interpretation, and the phenomenological perspective. I assume with Jones and Nisbett (1971) that actors typically attribute their own behavior to situational factors. Our witch-burning ancestors would have pointed to the mysterious death of cattle and the suspicious behavior of the old woman to explain their behavior. A naive situationist of the era might have identified the stimulus factors leading to witch burning as unexplained death of persons or domestic animals, and presence of a woman who lived alone and was old, poor, and a social isolate. The naive trait theorist might have looked for clinical-type trait aberrations in the burners—or in the witch. Only the phenomenologist would have pointed to the psychological situation—the occurrence of the external stimuli, the dying cattle, and friendless old woman—in a group atmosphere of belief in witches and consensus about what to do with them.

The case of the fainting ladies is even simpler. Again, the ladies themselves and a naive situationist would have agreed in attributing the fainting to the situation, the mention of the taboo body part. Obviously, since the mention of legs no longer causes fainting, we can now adopt the phenomenological perspective of attributing the fainting to the psychological characteristics of the situation, the fact that everyone "knew" that such topics were unthinkable and shocking to a proper lady, and that fainting was the natural response of ladies' weak nervous systems to the impact of such a shock. The Victorian trait theorist would, of course, have begun looking for individual differences in the weakness of the female nervous system.

Goldberg's subjects who "saw" nonexistent differences in essays present a more interesting problem. No doubt, again, the subjects themselves would have attributed their behavior to the external situation. They would have seen their rating of the essay as determined by its actual quality. Our naive situationists would have trouble with this one. They could, of course, point to the differing situational stimuli, the sex of the alleged authors, but they could not explain why sex of author should influence judgment of essay quality. Again, it was not the objective situation but the actor's interpretation of it that accounted for the behavior. The differential ratings reflected an implicit belief system of the time that women were less competent than men.

In each of these examples, no amount of detailed description of the physical stimulus situation can explain the behavior. In each of them, the phenomenological analysis can account for behavior by recognizing the effect of actors' interpretations of the situation on their behavior. The influence of the actors' interpretations in these examples was not recognized by the actors themselves, would not usually be sought as an explanatory construct by trait theorists, and was certainly not predictable from knowledge of the external stimulus conditions alone.

Psychological Meaning of the Situation

I have argued that an explicit phenomenological analysis that recognizes subjects' roles in constucting their experience accounts for behavior more adequately than either the simple situationist or trait approaches. I also contend that applying the same phenomenological analysis to our own behavior as psychologists may shed further light on the controversy between situationists and trait theorists. At least part of this controversy derives from our tendency to blur the distinction between the control of behavior and the cause of behavior. Behavior can often be controlled by the stimulus conditions of the situation, the dying cattle and friendless old woman, the mention of legs, the attribution of female authorship. It is this kind of stimulus control of behavior that is so amply demonstrated in research to date. Understanding the causes of behavior is a different problem altogether. The understanding of causality is always a matter of interpretation. Bowers's (1973) discussion of this distinction deserves careful attention.

As Bowers pointed out, if you release the grip of your fingers from an apple you are holding, the apple falls; if you do not release your grasp, the apple does not fall. This is a highly reliable phenomenon. Our two experimental conditions, release and no release, produce clear and reliable differences in the behavior of the apple. Many of us are then seduced by the experimental method into concluding that releasing *causes* the falling. But even the more sophisticated analysis of context is incomplete. It is not merely releasing the apple in the context of the earth's gravitational field that causes the falling; we must also take account of the structure, the "personality" of the apple itself. If its internal structure were lighter than air, releasing it would cause it to float upward rather than fall downward. Obviously, given the relative consistency of the structure of apples and given that our concern is with apples located in the vicinity of the earth's surface, we can predict and control the behavior of apples by our grip-release variable. It is the step from prediction and control, on the one hand, to understanding of causality, on the other, that is problematic.

I do not mean to imply that psychologists do not know the difference between the control of behavior and the cause of behavior. Most personality researchers who work with R-R data and correlational designs learned long ago to renounce any formal claims to the prestigious turf of cause-and-effect relationships. Similarly, sophisticated situationists speak of controlling behavior or of functional relationships. Most of us know (when we think about it) that the link between behavior control data and an understanding of the causes of that behavior is "interpretation in terms of a theoretical context." But, just as we take for granted and forget the influence of subjects' interpretations of the situation on their behavior, so we also take for granted and forget our own role in interpreting our research data situation in constructing our understanding of causality. The result is that we slide imperceptibly and unintentionally from statements about the control of behavior to conclusions implying causality. Just as the phenomenological analysis requires us to recognize our subjects' active role in constructing their experience, it also requires us to recognize our own active interpreter role in constructing the science of psychology.

It may be this same blurring of the distinction between control and causality on our part that makes humanists object to "the image of man" (they mean the image of human beings, of course) they see us as promulgating. To the extent that we seem to claim that behavior is caused by situational variables, rather than claiming more accurately that it is controlled by them, we seem to eliminate human judgment and responsibility. Skinner (1971) has addressed this point explicitly, and so has Mischel (1973).

The importance of the situation as perceived by the person (whether in the role of subject, psychologist, or any other role) is a familiar lesson. In fact, the role of the person's perceptual construction of the situation may be so familiar that it may often be assumed, taken for granted—and forgotten—by situationists, in the same way that the situation has often been forgotten by trait theorists.

PERSONALITY AS A NONCONSCIOUS PROCESS

A major implication of the phenomenological analysis is that most people are not aware of all of the causes of their own behavior. Typically, the external causes are recognized but not the internal ones. In the terminology used above, we are aware of the situational factors that control our behavior but not the internal, organizing principles through which we view and interpret the situation. This argument is as old as Freud. In all of the examples mentioned in this chapter—witch burners, fainting ladies, evaluators discriminating against female authors, and Rosenthal's experimenters and teachers—the persons involved would have attributed their behavior to the external situational factors, and they were not aware of the influence of their own beliefs and expectations on their behavior.

The Actor's Perception through Campbell's Downstream Periscope

Campbell's (1963) analysis of perception in terms of Hullian learning theory provides a theoretical explanation for this assertion. The main point of Campbell's argument is that the drive factors of the organism and the incentive value (meaning, significance) of the stimulus to the organism influence what the organism sees before it is aware of seeing it. Our conscious perception is not of "the real world out there" as it comes to us through our sense organs. Rather, our consciousness of the incoming sensory data occurs "downstream," after the incoming flow has been processed through our neural association areas. That is, our sense data have already been filtered through our needs, values, prejudices, fears, memories, beliefs, expectations, and cognitive processing apparatus in general, *before* we become conscious of them. The problem is that we all feel that we have an upstream periscope, that our conscious perception is a veridical representation of the external world. We misperceive the meanings we use to construe the situation as attributes of the situation itself.

Using this model of perception in his analysis of stereotyping, Campbell (1967) argued that although prejudiced people believe that their hostility toward minority group members is caused by the group's unpleasant behavioral habits (a naive situationist explanation), in fact, the hostility comes first, and it is only because of the preexisting hostility that a negative stereotype (a label with negative connotations) is attached to the group's behavioral habits. Behavior that is considered flexible and cooperative in our friends can easily be seen as wishy-washy and spineless in our enemies.

Campbell's analysis, applied to our perceptions of our own behavior, yields the following paradigm: We see our own behavior as actors as determined largely by the external situation;

we also see our perception of the external situation as veridical. What we fail to see is that our perception of the situation has already been influenced by our needs, fears, assumptions, and so forth, before we ever become conscious of it. These factors that influence our perception without our awareness might be called idiosyncracies of past reinforcement history by situationists, or they might be called traits (if they operate consistently) by personality theorists.

The idea of behavior being influenced without awareness need not imply sinister Freudian dynamics. The same principle, exactly, operates in simple visual perception. If you ask me to what do I attribute my seeing a huge, magnificent, old maple tree when I look out my window, I will most likely answer that I see the tree because it is there, growing right in front of my window. Few people would mention the structure or functioning of their eyeballs, much less their central nervous system neurons and synapses. We do not see our eyeballs when we look at a tree because we are not looking *at* them but by means of them. We do not see our personality traits when they influence our behavior, in the same way that we do not see our eyeballs when we look at a tree.

The Observer's Perspective on the Actor's Personality

The personality-eyeball analogy can be pushed one step further. As Jones and Nisbett (1971) pointed out, an observer is more likely than the actor to attribute actors' behavior to their personality traits. Similarly, an observer is more likely to notice the role of the actor's eyeballs in seeing the tree. Thus, while Jones and Nisbett thought the observer erred, I think (with Bowers, 1973) that actors also err. The observer has the advantage of perspective. For the observer, the actor's eyeballs, as well as the tree, are external and likely to be perceived. Similarly, observers have the perspective of their own personalities from which to notice the effects of the actor's personality.

Kelley and Stahelski's (1970) analysis of persons who are characteristically competitive in prisoners'-dilemma games illustrates the advantage of the observer's perspective. Early prisoners'-dilemma studies frequently concluded by mentioning large individual differences in styles of play. Some dyads fall into patterns of increasing competition over the course of play; others gradually evolve stable systems of mutual cooperation. Kelley and Stahelski studied two individual styles, a tendency to compete and a tendency to cooperate. When two competitors are paired they compete; when two cooperators are paired they cooperate. But when a cooperator is paired with a competitor, the results are the same as for two competitors. This is because cooperators are cooperative, not masochistic. They will cooperate with a cooperative partner but retaliate against a competitive opponent.

Kelley and Stahelski found that these subjects' perceptions of their social environment were congruent with their styles of play. Competitors see the world as populated by competitors. Cooperators see the world as populated by a mixture of cooperators and competitors. If a competitor and cooperator are paired, the competitor, expecting any partner to be competitive, begins competitively. Competitors may even see the initial cooperative plays of potential cooperators as attempts to lure them into exploitable vulnerability. Since they "know" the other is basically competitive, they continue to compete. The potential cooperator then gradually changes to increasing retaliation to avoid being exploited. As the cooperator plays more competitively in the face of the continuing competition, this "proves" to the competitive partner that his view of others as "all competitive" was justified after all.

In situations such as the one just outlined, competitive actors attribute their behavior to the external stimulus conditions, the competitiveness of the other person. What the competitors fail to see is the influence of their own personalities in creating those conditions. The actors' personalities have influenced their perceptions and through them their actions without their awareness of the influence. The result is an error on the actors' part in attributing their behavior to external stimulus conditions. In this case, only an observer with a perspective unavailable to the actors could notice the actual contingencies involved and the actors' own unknowing roles in creating them.

This does not say that observers' judgments of a subject's personality are correct. Implicit personality theories of the judge (Cronbach, 1955) may distort subjects' judgments of one another's personalities. The professional observations of personality psychologists may be distorted by their explicit personality theories as well as by their implicit theories. Nor does it say that observers have the whole story. With their focus on the figure of the actor, they may often fail to notice relevant details of the stimulus background. Campbell's (1967) prejudiced people are a good example of both actor error and observer error. As actors they err in failing to see the role of their own hostility in causing their negative stereotypes of the outgroup. As observers they err in attributing outgroup members' behavior to inborn personality traits and fail to see the influence of the outgroup's stimulus conditions of poverty, hostility, and discrimination. What I am arguing is that the influence of actors' personalities on their behavior is more likely to be visible to an observer (whether correctly or incorrectly interpreted) than to the actors themselves.

Summary of the Two Perspectives

Our personality traits influence our behavior largely without our conscious awareness. Although we attribute our behavior to the situation, we fail to see that our perception of the situation has already been influenced by our needs, fears, expectations, and past learning. In effect, we perceive the meanings we have used to construe the situation as attributes of the situation itself. This is because we do not perceive our own internal neural-cognitive processing of incoming sensory data; we only perceive consciously the results of that processing. The results are our conscious perception of the situation. Although we think we see "what is out there," actually we see our own interpretation of what is out there. An observer is more likely to notice actors' personality influences than the actors are, because actors' personalities are external to observers, who have the perspective of their own, different, construction systems. The result is that actors and naive situationists focus on the stimulus conditions that control behavior and lack the perspective required to perceive the effects of the actor's personality. On the other hand, observers and trait theorists focus on the person of the actor and often fail to notice the relevance of situational details.

IMPLICATIONS FOR BEHAVIORAL RESEARCH

The phenomenological analysis suggests three implications for personality research that have not been widely recognized:

1. We are more likely to find significant personality effects through the eyes of observers than in the self-reports of actors.
2. Actors' personalities are more visible when subjects are cognitively active than when they are passive or reactive.
3. Paper-and-pencil personality tests that use self-report, trait-descriptive items will relate to other behavior problematically, at best.

Detecting the Actor's Personality through the Observer's Perspective

If an observer is more likely than the actor to see the effects of the actor's personality, it follows that if we want to look for behavioral effects of personality, a logical place to find them is in the responses of another person. That is, make the personality of one person a stimulus condition for another.

Experimenters as Actors In fact, there may be a substantial body of statistically significant evidence of such personality effects that seldom appears in the journals. I am referring to effects associated with the particular persons serving as experimenters or stooges in our studies. As careful experimenters, many of us routinely guard against experimenter and stooge personality effects by having several different persons serve in our experimenter and stooge roles in each study. Naturally, the experimenter and stooge persons are carefully counterbalanced across experimental conditions. If it is our own research, we may stop there. If it is our graduate student's research, pedagogical concern may require entering experimenter persons and stooge persons in the analysis of variance. Those who have traveled this road know that effects of experimenters' and stooges' personalities are often statistically evident in the subjects' responses, either as main effects or in interactions with other variables.

For example, in a pilot study a few years ago a graduate student was measuring how close a subject would allow a male stranger to approach before asking him to stop. Two undergraduate men were recruited to serve as approaching strangers. They were carefully trained to give identical, standardized performances. The line of approach was physically marked on the floor; the approach was standardized for number of steps, size of steps, rate of stepping (and therefore total time taken to approach a given distance), facial expression, and eye contact with the waiting subject. In spite of this extensive training to equate the physical aspects of their performances, there was a significant effect for person of assistant. One of the men was allowed closer than the other, across all situational conditions. Since both assistants had been recruited from an undergraduate personality course in which Christie's (1970) Mach scales had been administered, it was possible to extrapolate a post hoc prediction from Mach theory. As surmised, when the assistants' Mach scores were examined, there was a large difference between them, and it was the low-Mach assistant who was allowed closer. Unfortunately, a formal test of this prediction, which requires at least two low-Mach approachers and two high Machs, has yet to be undertaken.

Fortunately, Marquis (1973) has reported a similar type of study using a different personality variable, authoritarianism. She had a persuasive message, a brief paragraph, read verbatim by an experimenter to a subject. Experimenters were drawn from a population pretested on Christie's (Christie, Havel, & Seidenberg, 1958) revision of the *F* scale. Three high-authoritarian experimenters participated, three low-authoritarians, and three yeasayers (subjects who agree with both authoritarian and reversed statements on the *F* scale). Each experimenter administered the persuasive treatment to nine subjects, and the experimenter personality effects were significant. High-authoritarian experimenters produced less attitude change than either low-authoritarians or yeasayers across all subjects.

Typically, we do not analyze our experimenters' personalities, so we have no idea what characteristics might be causing the observed effects. And since we counterbalance experimenters and stooges across conditions, we average across these person effects and avoid reporting inexplicable and irrelevant data. As

Bowers (1973) pointed out, we study situational effects by observing a few definably different situations across a large group of theoretically equivalent persons. If we want to find personality effects, perhaps we need to study a few definably different personality characteristics across a large group of theoretically equivalent situations.

Subjects as Actors Although the experimenter personality-effect paradigm fits Bowers's suggestion, there may be a more efficient way to observe personality variables in their role as situational conditions. That is to adopt an experimental design that might be called a fixed-effects version of Brunswik's (1955) stimulus-sampling design. Brunswik was concerned with traditional visual perception, but his ideas can also be applied to perception of personality. He argued that a valid study of perception must sample from the population of stimulus objects as well as from the population of subjects. This idea can be adapted to sampling from a population of stimulus persons (e.g., a population pretested on the personality variable of interest). In this design, subjects interact with each other, and responses are then examined for effects of having had a partner who was high versus low on the personality trait dimension. Although experimenters might sample randomly, a more efficient design would be to assign equal numbers of high- and low-scoring subjects to either high- or low-scoring partners.

Using a variation of such a design, Braginski (1970) asked high- and low-Mach children to persuade a middle-Mach child to eat quinine-soaked crackers. The effect of the persuader's Machiavellianism was clearly evident in the targets' responses—the number of crackers eaten. The juvenile high Machs' persuasive attempts produced twice as much cracker eating as did those of their low-Mach counterparts.

Novgorodoff (1974) used a more complex version of this same strategy to study Machiavellianism and romantic choices. He had subjects interact in groups of 12. Each group had three high-Mach men and three lows, and three high- and three low-Mach women. Thus, subjects' premeasured and definably different degrees of Machiavellianism served as the contrasted stimulus conditions, with effects clearly discernible in opposite-sex subjects' romantic preferences. In this nontask situation, low-Mach women were preferred by men in general, and especially by low-Mach men. And these same low-Mach women found the low-Mach men more romantically attractive than the high-Mach men. High-Mach women, on the other hand, preferred high-Mach men.

In this same study all subjects were rated for physical attractiveness by male and female high- and low-Mach experimental assistants. There were no Mach differences in subjects' physical attractiveness in these observer ratings. However, there were Mach effects in subjects' ratings of each other's physical attractiveness. These ratings generally paralleled the romantic attractiveness results. Evidently, there was a difference in the psychological meaning of the situation (in this study the psychological meaning of the stimulus person) for the experimental assistants and the participating subjects. The assistants rated the subjects as objects, through one-way mirrors, with no voice contact or personal interaction cues; their ratings were designed to be a pure visual impact measure. In contrast, the subjects rated each other after two sessions (totaling three hours) of increasingly unstructured, open-ended interaction with each other. Evidently the subjects' personalities influenced not only their romantic attractiveness but their apparent physical attractiveness as well.

So far, I have been suggesting that effects of actors' personalities may be more detectable in observers' responses than in actors' self-reports. The experimental paradigm outlined requires observers only to respond to the actor, not to judge or describe the actor's personality. In this paradigm, the accuracy of the observer's impressions of the actor is not an issue. The peer-rating literature represents a somewhat different paradigm in which accuracy is the major concern. In this literature observers are often more accurate in detecting actors' personality characteristics than the actors are in describing themselves. For example, Tupes and Christal (1961) found that peer ratings predicted military success better than self-ratings. Hirschberg (1977) found that peer ratings among graduate students predicted later success (grades, completing a degree, publishing, etc.) far better than self-reports.

Catching Personality in the Act

If subjects, partners, and other observers are such sensitive detectors of another's personality, how can we explain the disappointing results of years of research in person perception in which subjects were often asked to guess personality characteristics of target persons and typically succeeded so minimally that the overall results must be classified as a failure? A possible answer is provided by the phenomenological analysis. In this analysis, personality is an action process; it is the pattern of consistencies in the way we organize and construe sense data into meaningful situations in the process of perceiving and responding. In most of the earlier person-perception research, the target persons were seen by the subjects only in passive roles. Still photographs of the target persons were often used as stimuli. At best, subjects were shown sound movies of the target person being interviewed. But even in these movie studies (e.g., Cline & Richards, 1960) the target persons were psychologically passive and reactive; it was the interviewer who was actively structuring the situation. The phenomenological analysis would predict that if different interviewers as well as different interviewees were used in the stimulus movies, interviewer personality would have stronger effects than interviewee personality on subjects' responses. It may be noteworthy that all of these examples of subjects who responded differently to others with differing personalities involved the others in playing active roles in creating and structuring the situations in which the subjects observed them.

Mischel (1973) has argued that to observe personality effects in the laboratory, the situations must be weakly rather than powerfully defined by the experimenter. Under the present analysis, the question is not so much how powerfully the experimenter defines the situation, but rather how active the definition requires subjects to be. I am arguing that subjects must be active in structuring the situation for personality effects to emerge. Although there may be a negative correlation between how powerfully the experimenter defines the situation and the degree of subjects' activity, a weak experimenter definition does not guarantee active structuring by subjects; neither does a powerful experimenter definition prevent it.

For example, effects of subjects' Machiavellianism were clearly evident in a bargaining-coalition game (Geis, 1970) in which the situation as a whole was powerfully defined as a game. The game structure and playing rules provided further strong definitions of specific details of the situation. Players' resources were explicitly defined by assigned hands of playing cards, and the bargaining and coalition rules further defined the possibilities for action. Yet, the situation created by this network of powerful definitions was one that elicited active construing and responding by the players.

In order to win, subjects usually had to negotiate an agreement with a fellow player that required both partners to contribute resources to achieve the payoff neither could achieve alone. But such coalitions were only permitted, not required. Subjects had to decide whether to try to initiate a coalition and, if so, with which of two possible partners, or whether to accept a particular coalition offer from a particular fellow player at that particular time in the game. Prospective partners had to agree on how they would divide the joint payoff if their coalition won. This negotiation involved a delicate counter-balancing of their respective resources, their relative positions on the playing board at the time, and a less definable factor that might be called "what the traffic, at the moment, would bear." Since coalitions could be made and broken throughout the game, subjects had to construe the situation and initiate action when and if they could, in the context of an ongoing social interaction. Basically, this was a manipulation game. The winners were those who were most successful in exploiting others. In this situation, in which subjects were active, creative, and often ingenious, the correlation between personality as measured by Mach scores and number of points won in a six-game tournament was .71.

The effect of players' personalities was evident not only in the final game outcome but also in their responses to each other in the bargaining process. Players always had a choice of two possible coalition partners who (unknown to them at the time) differed in Mach score. Middle- and low-Mach players consistently preferred the high Mach as a partner, ignoring or rejecting offers from each other. If these players chose the high Mach because they expected him or her to help them more, they were grossly deceived. But regardless of their reasons, these participant-observers discriminated consistently between active actors who differed in personality.

In surveying the experimental research on Machiavellianism, Geis and Christie (1970) defined "latitude for improvisation" as one of three situational characteristics associated with behavioral differences between high and low scorers on the Mach Scale. Although this situational characteristic of requiring active structuring by subjects may be specific to detecting Machiavellianism, the phenomenological analysis that sees personality as characteristic habits of construction and response suggests that it should be relevant to all or most personality characteristics.

Implications for Personality Test Construction

A major implication of the downstream periscope model of perception is that people are only vaguely aware of their own personalities. Personality characteristics are mostly upstream processes that serve to shape our perceptions, and we are aware only of the results of the processing, not the processing principles themselves.

I do not mean to suggest that all personality traits are inaccessible; most are simply unnoticed. In fact, most people seem to have a peculiar dual system of believing they know their personality traits on the one hand, and trying to find out what their personality "really" is, on the other. People seem to have no trouble at all reporting on personality tests the extent to which they are happy, altruistic, cruel, independent, and so on. The problem is, what do their responses mean? (The average degree of happiness claimed in a national-sample survey some years ago was "happier than average!") On the other hand, the popularity of astrological character interpretations, and the eagerness with which students take personality tests and listen to the interpretations of their scores, suggest that most people are in fact uncertain about their true personality characteristics.

If people were accurately aware of their own personality traits, constructing a personality test would be simple. A test would need only one item giving an accurate description of the trait and asking subjects to locate themselves on a scale indicating the extent to which they possess it.

On the other hand, to the extent that personality is largely an upstream process operating outside of conscious awareness, it follows that constructing a personality test of items that ask subjects in various ways the extent to which they have the target trait is likely to yield more noise than signal. Three personality tests that have produced consistent behavioral predictions have in common the characteristic of avoiding this pitfall. Christie's (1970) Mach scale does not contain a single item asking subjects how much they manipulate others. Rather, the items ask about interpersonal strategies in general which people who are successful manipulators respond to differently from people who are not. The Marlowe-Crowne Scale of Need for Approval (Crowne & Marlowe, 1960) never asks subjects how dependent they are on social approval, how much they try to fake good, or how defensive they are. Instead, the items pit honesty against social desirability. Similarly, the Authoritarianism Scale (Adorno, Frenkel-Brunswik, Levinson, & Sanford, 1950) does not mention minority groups or ask subjects about their degree of prejudice. The trick seems to be to write nonreactive items that tap into subjects' downstream attitudes, beliefs, or perceptions that are correlated with their upstream (personality) locations on the trait dimension.

FRAGILITY OF PERSONALITY TRAITS IN THE LABORATORY: SOCIAL COMPARISON THEORY

Persons' awareness of their own personality, psychologists' attempts to detect it, and the massive impact of the situation in controlling laboratory behavior can now be considered from one final theoretical perspective. Personality traits may function like attitudes, opinions, and emotions in being susceptible to influence and redefinition by social comparison processes. This follows from the observation that most of us have no clear idea of our own traits. Even when we think we know our traits, which of them should be relevant to the particular situation is probably ambiguous at best. The details of this argument follow.

When the criterion for action or decision is ambiguous, we look for social cues. What I am proposing is that Festinger's (1954) social comparison theory may apply to personality traits as well as to opinions and emotions. Festinger originally proposed that when no clear physical criterion is available to test the truth of an opinion, social consensus serves as the criterion. Schachter (1959) extended this analysis to emotions and went on to argue (1964) the more general case that which emotion one experiences depends upon situational cues, often social ones. I propose to extend this same analysis to personality traits: when there is no clear physical criterion available to test whether we possess a certain trait, or how much of it we possess, we will use social consensus (e.g., others' expectations or definitions) as the criterion.

Rosenthal's (1974) analysis of experimenters' expectancies influencing subjects' behavior and teachers' expectancies influencing pupils was cited earlier from the experimenters' and teachers' point of view to illustrate the influence of intraperson cognitive processes in shaping perception of the social environment. From the point of view of the subjects and pupils, Rosenthal's demonstrations form a subcategory of social comparison theory. The subjects' and pupils' personality traits (characteristic attitudes, behaviors, performances, etc.) were influenced by others' beliefs and expectations.

If subjects' personality traits are as ambiguous to them as are the validity of their opinions and the appropriateness of their emotions, then it should not be surprising that so many personality traits dissolve so readily in situational cues. If subjects in dissonance research can be persuaded to choose "by their own free will" to perform actions contrary to their private beliefs, then subjects in personality research can certainly be persuaded by their perception of the situation to act contrary to their personalities.

An early study by Backman, Secord, and Pierce (1963) illustrates the effects of social comparison processes on subjects' definitions of their own personalities. As part of an extensive personality test battery, subjects were asked to rank the 15 traits from the Edwards Personal Preference Schedule (Edwards, 1959) in order of how characteristic the traits were of themselves. The subjects were then given a list of five significant others (mother, father, best friend, etc.) and asked to check the five Edwards traits each of these people would attribute to them. For each subject, one high-consensus trait was identified and one low-consensus trait. A high-consensus trait was one subjects had ranked second, third, or fourth on the self-rating and had indicated that significant others would also attribute to them. A low-consensus trait was one similarly ranked second, third, or fourth by subjects, but not marked as a likely attribution of most of the significant others. At a later session, subjects were given purported feedback on their personality test results. Each subject found one high-consensus trait and one low-consensus trait marked as highly *uncharacteristic.* Subjects were then asked to describe themselves again by rank ordering the Edwards' traits as before. As predicted, subjects showed more change on the low-consensus trait in the direction of the experimenter's situational definition than on the high-consensus trait. Recall that both high- and low-consensus traits had initially been ranked second, third, or fourth by the subjects themselves. The experimenter's social redefinition was strong enough to change subjects' estimates of their own personalities when the estimate was not supported by outside social consensus, but the manipulation had less effect against the competition of external social support.

Does this social comparison theory analysis merely affirm what situationists have been claiming—that traits (in the sense of enduring, consistent characteristics) are mostly a figment of the imaginations of personality researchers, college sophomores, and other erring observers? Not at all. The fact that we can modify or eliminate a psychological process in the laboratory does not disprove its existence outside of the laboratory. We can easily modify or eliminate vision in the laboratory by lenses, blindfolds, or surgical procedures. This does not indicate that vision is either imaginary or unimportant. The social comparison theory analysis is intended to apply to personality traits in general, but it is especially pertinent to the problem of researching personality in the laboratory. The same social comparison processes that help maintain consistency in personality traits outside of the laboratory serve to dissolve that consistency in the laboratory.

Outside of the laboratory, we typically know something about the situations we enter in terms of their meaning, their context, their purpose. Most extralaboratory situations are familiar. Our previous knowledge and expectations shape our perceptions and responses. These characteristic perceptions and responses are the behaviors that our friends see as our personality traits.

In familiar situations the ongoing social comparison processes (others' beliefs and expectations about our purposes and behaviors, and our beliefs and expectations about theirs) support our characteristic constructions and responses; at least we have learned to construe them as supporting. On the other hand, most laboratory situations provide little familiar context for subjects. They typically claim to feel uncertain of the meaning and purpose of procedures. (Although the experimenter has carefully explained the relevance of the procedure to the experiment, the subjects have not had a chance to construct the meaning and purpose of the situation to themselves.) In this ambiguous situation, with no relevant, previous experience of it, subjects look for external cues. Among the most salient of these are the experimenter's definitions. Thus, subjects put their own personalities in temporary abeyance, as it were, as they see the situation through the experimenter's definitions. And thus, the personality effects most visible in the statistical analysis are those of the experimenter rather than those of the subjects.

This peculiar effect of the laboratory on personality traits is similar to the laboratory effect on attitudes noted by Hovland (1959) years ago. He observed that while laboratory manipulation typically produced pervasive attitude change in the direction advocated, similar treatments outside of the laboratory produced virtually no effects at all. In both cases the story seems to be consistency outside the laboratory and inconsistency (easy change) in it.

The problem in personality research that is clarified by the social comparison analysis is that because subjects' personality traits are ambiguous to them, they are highly susceptible to alteration in novel and also ambiguous laboratory situations by experimenters' explicit or implicit demands, expectations, or cues. A possible solution to this problem might be to design laboratory situations that provide context and meaning cues that subjects experience as familiar. It was argued earlier that personality is an action process, the person's characteristic patterns of construing situations and responses. Feelings of familiarity would presumably facilitate those constructions that are characteristic of the person in that type of situation.

The importance of the person's feeling familiar with the situation in order for it to elicit personality effects has not been widely discussed in the literature. I know of no study testing this proposition; yet it seems to make sense. All of the situations cited in this essay in which actors' personalities were detectable were situations in which the actors in question were performing familiar roles or routines. As mentioned, effects of experimenters' personalities are more reliably detected than effects of subjects' personalities in most laboratory research. The experimenters are the ones who are familiar with the situation. Rosenthal (1974) cited an unpublished study by Marwit showing that the effect of experimenters' expectancies on subjects' Rorschach performances was greater for subjects contacted later. Apparently, the experimenters came to dominate and define the situation more powerfully as they gained experience and familiarity with it.

The requirement of a specifically familiar situation is probably too simplistic (although this is undoubtedly an advantage of field studies). Human subjects bring powerful symbolizing-analogizing abilities to the laboratory. A situation that evokes familiar psychological-meaning parameters may also elicit the characteristic construction effects.

For example, the bargaining-coalition game mentioned earlier was developed specifically for the study of Machiavellianism (Geis, 1970) in which it was used. None of the subjects had ever played that exact game before. Neither was the game a replica of such familiar life situations as candidate job interviewing, getting out of doing the dishes, picking up the tab in a restaurant, or getting a group to adopt one's own proposal over alternative proposals of opponents. Rather, the game created psychological-meaning parameters common to these and a host of other familiar situations. The game structure provided context and meaning cues that created a psychological situation familiar to the subjects, the situation of fair exchange for mutual benefit. The specific decisions involved were familiar types of decisions in this kind of situation—which of the available partners to ally with, how much payoff to demand for oneself or offer to the other, whether to keep an existing agreement or break it for a better deal with someone else. Presumably this familiar situation of fair exchange for mutual benefit elicited subjects' (differing) characteristic expectancies, standards of reasonableness of agreements, and interpersonal strategies. As noted previously, the effect of Machiavellianism was evident. The high Machs parlayed their share of the mutual benefits into twice the size of the low Machs' share.

This social comparison analysis of personality traits also provides some support for psychotherapy. From the point of view of social comparison theory, psychotherapy is a social comparison process in which patients gradually come to accept and internalize the therapist's redefinition of their personality traits—their characteristic construction and response habits. Typically, the patient does most of the talking: because personality is an active construction process, the patient can learn the new constructions only by rehearsing them actively. Lengthy therapies are an indication of the amount of time it takes to develop the experiental basis for the new traits. Group therapies may be effective because, although the patient spends less time actively rehearsing, the group provides a more powerful social consensus supporting the redefinitions. The groups, however, need not be large. In the Asch (1956) studies, groups of three produced maximum conformity to the consensus. The social comparison analysis also implies that therapy cannot be independent of the therapist's values and expectations (or the therapist's biases and prejudices). These are the redefinitions learned by the patient. Thus, for years women patients of Freudian analysts learned to renounce the clitoris and have vaginal orgasms, until Masters and Johnson (1966) told us there was no such thing. In the more fortunate cases, the therapist's redefinitions probably are an improvement over the patient's previously inadequate, self-defeating patterns.

Bem and Allen (1974) argued that some persons are more consistent than others in expressing a given personality trait. It seems equally likely that some personality traits should be more "situation soluble" than others (Bowers, 1973). Traits like friendliness and generosity seem subject to voluntary regulation and therefore especially susceptible to redefinition by social comparison processes. Such traits may be more situation specific, while others may be less readily altered at will, like dependency, defensiveness, or the ability traits suggested by Mischel (1973). Most personality traits probably fall between these extremes. They operate in situations in which familiar psychological parameters elicit characteristic construction and response habits; they dissolve readily in unfamiliar laboratory situations in which subjects look for situational cues in experimenters' definitions; and they become invisible when subjects are passive.

PERSONALITY TRAITS AS SCRIPTS

Most trait psychologists would agree that our history of situations shapes our personality traits, and most situationists would agree that situations are created and maintained by the personalities (broadly construed) of the participants. Such agreements might seem to argue for the interactionist approach advocated by Bowers (1973) and Cronbach (1975). But the prospect of looking for more and more ever higher order interactions among more and more highly differentiated trait and situation variables is probably tedious enough to cool the ardor of most researchers. After Cronbach (1955) explained the complexities required for adequate person-perception research, that line of research effectually terminated. After a brief hiatus, the problem was approached from a new perspective, attribution theory.

The present problem of traits and situations similarly may need a new approach. One possibility is taking a more global approach, selecting a larger, more organized system as the unit of analysis. This approach would see the person and the situation as a unitary system. As required by the phenomenological analysis, the situation could be said to be in the person as much as the person could be said to be in the situation. Our previous attempts to describe personality in terms of pure, elementary trait particles may be analogous to trying to describe a person's appearance by specifying the length of the nose in centimeters, the distance between the centers of the eyes, the average number of hairs per eyebrow, and so forth. Although the details may be correct, what we are after is not simply the sum of its parts; it is by nature (in terms of our common perceptual habits) a gestalt, an organized whole. Analogously, personality is the person–situation interaction system seen as a whole.

Systems theorists tend to claim that a system cannot be understood by studying its components separately. A component separated from the system does not have the same function or the same meaning that it has within the system. Although there is certainly some truth to this argument, I am not sure it applies to personality. It seems equally likely that each level of analysis has its own meaning and its own validity (Fiske makes a strong case for this point in Chap. 2). There must certainly be a legitimate study of situation components and an equally legitimate study of construction process and outcome components. These are, of course, the traditional subareas of psychology. The question is the extent to which personality is simply the sum of its components versus the extent to which its system characteristics make it a qualitatively different phenomenon.

One example of a shift in focus to a larger, more organized system is Abelson's (1976) script theory of attitudes. According to Abelson, attitudes in the sense of simple elementary cognitive particles that psychologists have previously been studying have little consistent meaning or function in people's behavior outside of laboratory experiments. What he proposed is that functionally significant attitudes outside of the laboratory come in scripts. Perhaps personality traits also come in scripts. A script is a scenario, like a cartoon, a comic strip, or a TV commercial, with both visual and verbal elements, a picture with caption. For example, a person may favor equal opportunity for all in a script for expressing (abstract) beliefs about America, democracy, and so on. That person may oppose equal funding for girls' and boys' athletic programs in the local high school in a script for serving as a member of the Board of Trustees (and local football fan) deciding on next year's high school budget allocations. Scripts may be short, one-scene representations, or they may be long, sequential, and complex. Most of us have a script for saying, "How are you?" upon encountering a casual acquaintance. We may also have a script, much more complex and highly differentiated, for developing a lifetime career. But any script is always an organized whole. It is always a "person in a situation as perceived by the person."

The script deals directly with experience, the amalgam of person and situation required by the phenomenological analysis. It specifies the situation in terms of its meaning to the person; it specifies the person's experience or response in terms of his or her construal of the meaning of the situation. Some jokes and cartoons derive their humor from disruptions of familiar scripts, from portraying a logical but unconventional construction of a familiar script. The script notion satisfies the phenomenological analysis of personality traits as active construction processes. The script presents the situation specifically in terms of its construction, its meaning to the actor. And, of course, the script interpretation of personality functioning also satisfies the familiarity requirement. The idea that a person has a script for a situation implies that the situation is a familiar one to the person. Finally, the study of behavior in terms of scripts insures that neither situation or personality can be omitted from the analysis; the script is the person-situation interaction system, seen as a whole. Perhaps personality might be viewed as the playing out of particular scripts that a person characteristically resorts to in familiar situations.

REFERENCES

Abelson, R. P. Script processing in attitude formation and decision-making. In J. S. Carroll & J. W. Payne (Eds.), *Cognition and social behavior.* New York: Erlbaum, 1976.

Adorno, T. W., Frenkel-Brunswik, E., Levinson, D. J., & Sanford, R. N. *The authoritarian personality.* New York: Harper & Row, 1950.

Asch, S. E. Studies of independence and conformity. A minority of one against a unanimous majority. *Psychological Monographs,* 1956, *70*(9, Whole No. 416).

Backman, C. S., Secord, P. F., & Pierce, J. R. Resistance to change in the self-concept as a function of consensus among significant others. *Sociometry,* 1963, *26,* 102–111.

Bem, D. J., & Allen, A. On predicting some of the people some of the time: The search for cross-situational consistencies in behavior. *Psychological Review,* 1974, *81,* 506–520.

Bowers, K. S. Situationism in psychology: An analysis and a critique. *Psychological Review,* 1973, *80,* 307–336.

Braginski, D. D. Machiavellianism and manipulative interpersonal behavior in children. *Journal of Experimental Social Psychology,* 1970, *6,* 77-99.

Bruner, J. S. Personality dynamics and the process of perceiving. In R. S. Blake & G. V. Ramsey (Eds.), *Perception, an approach to personality.* New York: Ronald, 1951.

Brunswik, E. Representative design and probabilistic theory in a functional psychology. *Psychological Review,* 1955, *62,* 193-217.

Campbell, D. T. Social attitudes and other acquired behavioral dispositions. In S. Koch (Ed.), *Psychology: A study of a science* (Vol. 6). New York: McGraw-Hill, 1963.

Campbell, D. T. Stereotypes and the perception of group differences. *American Psychologist,* 1967, *22,* 817-829.

Christie, R. Scale construction. In R. Christie & F. L. Geis, *Studies in Machiavellianism.* New York: Academic Press, 1970.

Christie, R., Havel, J., & Seidenberg, B. Is the *F*-scale irreversible? *Journal of Abnormal and Social Psychology,* 1958, *56,* 143-159.

Cline, V. B., & Richards, J. M., Jr. Accuracy of interpersonal perception—A general trait? *Journal of Abnormal and Social Psychology,* 1960, *60,* 1-7.

Cronbach, L. J. Processes affecting scores on "understanding of others" and "assumed similarity." *Psychological Bulletin,* 1955, *52,* 177-193.

Cronbach, L. J. Beyond the two disciplines of scientific psychology. *American Psychologist,* 1975, *30,* 116-127.

Crowne, D. P., & Marlowe, D. A new scale of social desirability independent of psychopathology. *Journal of Consulting Psychology,* 1960, *24,* 349-354.

Edwards, A. L. *Edwards Personal Preference Schedule.* New York: Psychological Corporation, 1959.

Festinger, L. A theory of social comparison processes. *Human Relations,* 1954, *7,* 117-140.

Geis, F. L. The con game. In R. Christie and F. L. Geis, *Studies in Machiavellianism.* New York: Academic Press, 1970.

Geis, F. L., & Christie, R. Overview of experimental research. In R. Christie & F. L. Geis, *Studies in Machiavellianism.* New York: Academic Press, 1970.

Goldberg, P. Are women prejudiced against women? *Trans-action,* April 1968, *5,* 28-30.

Hirschberg, N. Predicting the performance of graduate students. In M. Kaplan & S. Schwartz (Eds.), *Human judgment and decision processes: Applied aspects.* New York: Academic Press, 1977.

Hovland, C. I. Reconciling conflicting results derived from experimental and survey studies of attitude change. *American Psychologist,* 1959, *14,* 8-17.

Jones, E. E., & Nisbett, R. E. The actor and the observer: Divergent perceptions of the causes of behavior. In E. E. Jones, D. E. Kanouse,

H. H. Kelley, R. E. Nisbett, S. Valins, & B. Weiner (Eds.), *Attribution: Perceiving the causes of behavior.* Morristown, N.J.: General Learning Press, 1971.

Kelley, H. H., & Stahelski, A. J. The inference of intention from moves in the prisoner's dilemma game. *Journal of Experimental Social Psychology,* 1970, *6,* 401–419.

Lewin, K. *Principles of topological psychology.* New York: McGraw-Hill, 1936.

Marquis, P. C. Experimenter-subject interaction as a function of authoritarianism and response set. *Journal of Personality and Social Psychology,* 1973, *25,* 289–296.

Masters, W. H., & Johnson, V. E. *Human sexual response.* Boston: Little, Brown, 1966.

Mischel, W. *Personality and assessment.* New York: Wiley, 1968.

Mischel, W. Toward a cognitive social learning reconceptualization of personality. *Psychological Review,* 1973, *80,* 252–283.

Murray, H. A. *Explorations in personality.* New York: Oxford Press, 1938.

Novgorodoff, B. Boy meets girl: Machiavellianism and romantic attraction. Paper presented at the Annual Meetings of the American Psychological Association, New Orleans, La., September 1974.

Postman, L. Towards a general theory of cognition. In J. A. Rohrer & M. Sherif (Eds.), *Social psychology at the crossroads.* New York: Harper, 1951.

Rosenthal, R. *On the social psychology of the self-fulfilling prophecy: Further evidence for Pygmalion effects and their mediating mechanisms.* New York: MSS Modular Publications, 1974.

Sarason, I. G., Smith, R. E., & Diener, E. Personality research: Components of variance attributable to the person and the situation. *Journal of Personality and Social Psychology,* 1975, *32,* 199–204.

Schachter, S. *The psychology of affiliation: Experimental studies of the sources of gregariousness.* Stanford, Calif.: Stanford University Press, 1959.

Schachter, S. The interaction of cognitive and physiological determinants of emotional state. In L. Berkowitz (Ed.), *Advances in experimental social psychology.* New York: Academic Press, 1964.

Skinner, B. F. *Beyond freedom and dignity.* New York: Knopf, 1971.

Tupes, E. C., & Christal, R. E. Recurrent personality factors based on trait ratings. *USAF ASD Technical Report,* 1961, No. 61–67.

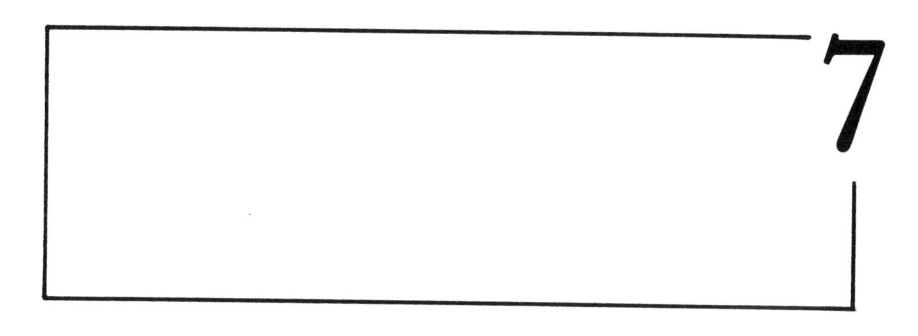

PERSONALITY: PARADIGMS AND POLITICS

HARVEY LONDON
New School for Social Research

This collection of papers was intended, at least in part, to evaluate the impact of traits and situations on behavior. Some investigators have focused upon the trait as a key determinant of behavior (cf., London & Exner, 1978); others have focused upon the situation (e.g., Barker, 1968). The field of experimental personality research seems to be moving toward the position (Endler & Magnusson, 1976; Magnusson & Endler, 1977) that both traits and situations are key constructs and most important when they interact to predict behavior.

It is sobering to realize that many years ago Kurt Lewin claimed that Behavior (B) is a function of the Person (P) in interaction with the Environment (E). I say sobering for obvious reasons: Lewin's formulation is virtually synonymous with the

This paper has profited from conversations with John Exner, Richard Pollinger, David Schneider, Sidney Stecher, and Stuart Valins.

interactionist position mentioned above. This has been pointed out by Carlson (1975) and by Ekehammar (1974). The papers throughout this book represent, for the most part, one of the positions cited: an emphasis on the trait, on the situation, or on both trait and situation. For my part, I would like to introduce another way of conceptualizing the area.

First, consider Lewin's formula, $B = f(P, E)$. It is interesting that when Lewin stated his formula, he argued his case on theoretical grounds. I doubt that Lewin ever tried to measure a trait. I'm certain he never partitioned behavioral variance into variance caused by persons and variance caused by environment. Although recent researchers (Bowers, 1973; Golding, 1975; Sarason, Smith, & Diener, 1975) have studied Lewin's equation empirically, the concepts were initially based on theory.

It took Mischel's critique of personality research to reawaken interest in Lewin's formulation. That formulation, like the heredity-versus-environment issue, has become a paradigm (Kuhn, 1962) for personality research. Whether the paradigm will provide a significant contribution to personality research is a major concern of the papers in this book.

AN ADDITION TO LEWIN'S FORMULA

A central question in this chapter is whether a theoretical term should be added to the simple Lewinian formula. The research of at least one psychologist, Stanley Schachter, suggests the importance of an additional construct in the theoretical network.

Schachter began his professional life as a fairly orthodox Lewinian, carrying out field research employing group dynamics concepts (Festinger, Schachter, & Back, 1950), later involving himself in studies (e.g., Festinger, Riecken, & Schachter, 1956) inspired by his colleague Leon Festinger, also a Lewinian.

The watershed in Schachter's career came with his work on affiliation (Schachter, 1959) in which he argued that there was reason to believe that people affiliate, at least in part, in order to gain insight into their feelings. In other words, cognitive factors seemed important determinants of emotions.

At this point, Schachter made a conceptual leap that was,

in a way, quite daring for a social psychologist in the Lewinian tradition. He knew that investigators of emotion had expended a great deal of energy attempting, without much success, to understand emotions on the basis of physiological variables alone. He believed that the situation would be rectified by adding cognition as a determinant of emotion; so he embarked on a series of experiments that demonstrated the importance of both physiological arousal and cognition (labeling) in explaining emotion. The result was Schachter's (1971) cognitive-physiological theory of emotion. The theory states that emotions are a function of the interaction of physiological arousal and cognitions (i.e., one's label for one's arousal). This formulation was tested in a variety of ways, including an experiment (Schachter, 1971, Chap. 1) in which a biological agent (epinephrine or placebo) was one variable and a set of cognitions was another.

Schachter's theory of emotion predicts that emotion will occur when people are physiologically aroused and emotion-relevant cognitions are available. Conversely, if they are not aroused, even if emotion-related cognitions are present, they will not experience emotion. If one formalizes Schachter's study in terms of Lewin's theoretical equation, the theory of emotion becomes: Behavior = *f*(Biology, Person). In formalizing Schachter's theory this way, I am distinguishing between the person described in terms of biological attributes and the person described in terms of mental state.

Application of Schachter's Theory

Work with more direct bearing on personality involved the application of Schachter's theory of emotion to a relatively emotionless type, the sociopath. Relevant to my position was an experiment (Schachter, 1971, Chap. 13) in which Schachter noted the differential effect of a biological agent (placebo or epinephrine) on normals and sociopaths in an avoidance learning task. Under placebo, normals learned to avoid pain, sociopaths did not. Under epinephrine, normals showed little change while sociopaths bettered their avoidance learning markedly.

Again, if we were to schematize Schachter's study in a Lewinian-type formula, we would have: Behavior = *f*(Biology, Person). This formula differs from the one used to represent

Schachter's theory of emotion since Person here stands for a stable individual difference variable.

The importance of biological variables is illustrated again in Schachter's work on obesity (Schachter, 1971; Schachter & Rodin, 1974). The theory guiding this research is based on a distinction between internal cues (physiological states) and external cues (situational states). It is assumed that the eating behavior of normals is largely under the control of internal cues (e.g. empty stomachs), while the eating behavior of the obese is largely under the control of external cues (e.g. quality of food). Most studies have confirmed these hypotheses and have shown how biological variables (like presence or absence of food in the stomach) interact with individual differences and/or environmental variables to affect eating behavior.

Schachter's work on emotion, sociopathy, and obesity suggests the necessity of adding the theoretical construct Biology to the Lewinian equation. Thus, Behavior = *f*(Biology, Person, Environment),[1] where Biology refers to physiological or biological states of the organism, Person refers to states of mind or individual differences, and Environment refers to external or situational characteristics. It is noted that physiological, or biological, variables are person variables but differ from states of mind or individual differences in that, among other things, they are constructs whose operational definitions are generally agreed upon and are usually measurable on an interval scale and sometimes, indeed, on a ratio scale. This is not to suggest they are more important in the Lewinian equation than are person variables, only that they usually have an empirical referent with greater construct validity.

Importance of Biological Variables

Although very few researchers in the fields of experimental social and personality psychology, other than Schachter, have manipulated biological variables, those who have consistently have shown the importance of these variables in their interaction with person and situational constructs in the prediction of behavior.

[1]This formula also appears in Ekehammar (1974). There, however, contrary to the principle of parsimony, no argument is given for the *necessity* of including Biology.

Although my revised Lewinian formula may appear simplistic on the surface, it should be noted that the independent variables would undoubtedly interact in complex ways in the determination of behavior. We might decide to distinguish among various types of person variables, such as the distinction Mischel has made between cognitive variables and trait variables. Physiological states sometimes may be observable and measurable, but in a theory of personality they might be hypothetical constructs.

At the very least, the formula I am suggesting as a paradigm for personality research represents a comprehensive taxonomy of variables affecting behavior. More important, the revised formula stresses the role of biological, or physiological, variables in our conceptualizations. Although the ultimate usefulness of this approach will be seen only in the research generated and the theories explaining such research, significant strides in this direction already have been noted.

Thus far, I have addressed a broader version of what might be called the interactional psychology issue. Interactional psychology (Endler & Magnusson, 1976; Magnusson & Endler, 1977) is a position that suggests a direction in which personality psychology should go. "Do not simply consider the person," the interactionists say. "Do not simply consider the situation. Consider both." To this formulation I add the construct of biology.

ANOTHER POSSIBLE DIRECTION FOR RESEARCH

Let us consider another possible direction in which personality research might go. Fiske (Chap. 2) has proposed that the field of personality become several sciences, each with its own approach. Following is a suggestion for one of Fiske's personality minisciences.

Several years ago a colleague at Brandeis University, vision psychologist Sidney Stecher, presented some aspects of the history of vision research that he thought might be relevant to personality. Roughly 40 years ago, vision research was in a state of disarray. Investigators from a variety of disciplines were working in the area but they worked from different theoretical bases. They defined their terms in different ways, and their data were not readily comparable. Thus, the research of those scientists was not and could not easily be synthesized for a more comprehensive understanding of vision.

But some vision researchers raised the possibility of standardizing the field. They suggested holding a conference of light scientists—people in optics, physics, psychology, illumination engineering, and other relevant fields—to see whether agreement on a unifying framework for research might be possible. Among their goals was the formation of working committees to arrive at agreed-upon, heuristic definitions of concepts.

That conference was held, and it began a series of meetings that continue to the present (e.g., National Research Council, 1975). The investigators decided on a framework for research that basically took the following form: Three statistically independent dimensions of light were considered important—wavelength, radiant intensity, and purity. The dimensions were not chosen randomly but were derived from the Young-Helmholtz theory of color vision. The researchers also decided to focus on a dependent variable which more or less flowed from their other decisions: light-matching behavior.

In light matching, the subject is presented with a field of light and three knobs, each of which controls one of the variables in the system. The subject adjusts the three knobs until a field looks the same as an adjacent lighted field. Other parameters considered important include size of the field and whether the field is focused on the center or periphery of the eye. The important point here is that a group of researchers decided to systematize the field by agreeing on the variables to be studied. According to Stecher, researchers agree that vision research has flourished under the system outlined.

Vision researchers are not the only scientific group to have organized their efforts. A group of respiratory physiologists have pledged themselves to a common set of definitions and symbols (Pappenheimer, 1950); the National Institute of Mental Health has established a depression section to initiate and coordinate collaborative research projects aimed at understanding depression and circumventing impediments to progress (Secunda, 1973). Other efforts include those of the Department of Health, Education and Welfare, which has established a unified problem classification system for children and youth, and the World Health Organization, which runs an International Reference Centers Network for Psychotropic Drugs.

It is a moot point whether the field of experimental personality research and, more specifically, trait-oriented personality research, is in as great a state of disarray today as vision research was 40 years ago. The new interactional personality psychology may be an improvement over older, simplistic trait theories in predicting behavior, but I do not think it will advance the field with regard to important biological variables to be considered or with regard to the structure and functioning of the "internal" system, undoubtedly comprised of both biological and person variables, which governs behavior.

One finds virtually no theoretical cohesion in personality research at present. One of the most popular strategies in experimental personality research has been to devise a single-concept trait measure and then to relate that measure to a variety of behaviors. As a result of this strategy, there are today approximately 13 important, or at least popular and influential, single-concept traits[2] (cf. London & Exner, 1978), each tied to its own operational measurement procedures and its own body of research. Certainly not all of the 13 traits are methodologically unsound. Despite his critique, Mischel himself (1976, p. 159) seemed to endorse the use of traits under certain conditions in experimental research.

What Shall We Do with the Traits?

What, then, shall we do with the 13 traits? If we do nothing, we shall almost certainly see the number of trait measures increase. I doubt that the addition of more traits will increase our knowledge, especially since we do not even have a viable theory of the traits already extant. I doubt also that researchers who believe traits to be useful constructs would consider their work finished

[2] It should be noted that the number 13 is obviously arbitrary. Cattell (1965) opted for 16 traits (possibly more today) to define the sphere of personality. Norman (1963) suggested 5; Leary (1957), 2; and Eysenck (Wilson, 1978), 3; but all of them have tended to devise "systems" of more than one trait.

even after they have compiled a "complete" catalogue (cf. Brody, 1972, p. 43) of traits. Rather, their work would have just begun. In fact, recent work on personality traits (Goldberg, 1977) has extended the original work by Norman (1963) and his associates in a direction relevant to my discussion. Whereas Norman delineated the realm of personality to be reproducible on the basis of five important trait dimensions, Goldberg enlarged the scope of this original research in an effort to develop a complete taxonomy of personality trait terms. This taxonomy includes not only all of the trait terms used in the English language to describe people, but also all of the important calibrations of the traits (e.g., social desirability, ambiguity, endorsement frequency). Goldberg even provided an heuristic, based on the distinction between the evaluative versus the descriptive aspect of the word, to generate word clusters that vary systematically in their social desirability. The primary question I would raise about this research is whether it is simply proliferating the number of trait terms that will be used by future researchers or whether the strategy underlying the research will generate a minitheory of traits. The answer to this question probably depends on the research strategy taken after the traits and their psychometric properties have been determined.

Some have counseled that we continue with the single-trait strategy for research. An approach that utilizes several personality concepts simultaneously has been advocated by Kelly (1967), who favors multivariate research designs, and Marlowe and Gergen (1969), who also argue for multivariate research designs and for multiple research strategies as well. Perhaps the time has come to bring a few of the traits into juxtaposition with one another.

TOWARD A MINISYSTEM OF PERSONALITY

A key aim of this paper is to explore the fruitfulness of bringing together experimental personality researchers for a purpose similar to that of the vision researchers of 40 years ago: (1) to choose a small number of personality measures from among all those available in order to study collaboratively the way in which those measures jointly operate to affect behavior, and (2) to form what might be called a definition-measurement-methodology committee to arrive at appropriate standardizations in those areas.

First, I must point out several things. Although I am partial to trait concepts, a standardized system of variables for experimental personality research does not require the use of traits alone or at all. Hirschberg (Chap. 3) has argued for the use of traits in conjunction with desires and beliefs. Geis (Chap. 6) has proposed "scripts" of personality variables, while Golding (Chap. 4) has suggested the use of psychological organizing principles. Dahlstrom (1972) advocated the use of traits in combination with dynamic variables; Mischel (1973) proposed the use of cognitive social learning person variables; I have suggested the importance of physiological variables. Thus, there are important conceptual issues to be dealt with before a multivariable personality system can be constructed.

Nor does the strategy I propose deny the importance of situations in the theoretical system. As my revised Lewinian formula suggests, the situation is crucial in its interaction with physiology and individual differences.

It must be acknowledged that systems, or systemlike schemes, have been proposed in the past by empirically oriented personality psychologists. Most of these systems have enjoyed little success in the programmatic development of the area. Two of the best known, those of Guilford (1959) and Cattell (1965), suffer from too much complexity and, in Cattell's case, from the use of neologisms to describe the important variables in the system. Personality, as conceptualized by both Guilford and Cattell, simply involves too many variables. Whatever their predictive status, the number of dimensions used by these men does not seem parsimonious enough to appeal to the experimentalist.

Eysenck's System

Perhaps the most familiar system of personality is that of Eysenck (Wilson, 1978). Eysenck postulates three dimensions of personality: introversion-extraversion; neuroticism-normality; and psychoticism-normality. Eysenck's scheme, which is far simpler than those of Guilford and Cattell, is perhaps the only system that has appealed to experimental personality psychologists. The fact that Eysenck's simple theory of personality has enjoyed so much success in generating empirical research supports my notion of turning to the intensive study of a few important variables considered jointly.

One important difference between Eysenck's scheme and my approach, patterned after the vision researchers, is that in my proposal the variables for study would be selected by experienced personality researchers acting collectively. Presumably, they would commit themselves as a group to performing research on the system formed by the chosen variables.

A community of personality researchers, acting collectively in an attempt to standardize not only measurement techniques but also the appropriate variables themselves, would, in my view, lead to progress in the field. An example of such a community can be seen in Henry Murray's group at Harvard in the 1930s. Such a community of scholars is also reminiscent of the old laboratories such as Wundt's in Germany.

There is, however, one major difference between the group of scholars working in vision research and those who might work in personality: vision scientists have had at their disposal a well-defined theory of vision. (Actually, they had more than one theory, but the point is that at least some sort of theoretical idea guided their research.) There is certainly no similarly esteemed or agreed-upon theory in personality. How, then, should variables be chosen? I have indicated that conceptual work would undoubtedly be involved in constructing the required system. How might the work be approached?

The most obvious method involves factor analysis: carry out a factor analysis of contending concepts and choose according to an appropriate criterion. In fact, the factor analytic approach is one that has been taken by most of the major trait-personality theorists [Cattell, 1965; Eysenck (Wilson, 1978); Guilford, 1959; Leary, 1957; Schutz, 1967]. This approach is superficially appealing because it does represent a parsimonious means for describing important trait words. However, it has a number of defects. Overall (1964) has shown that factor analysis in no way indicates which variables are basic. Factor analysis alone does not indicate which personality variables or dimensions would have predictive or construct validity, and it does not provide a guiding theoretical framework. Further, it may be relevant that there are well-researched personality concepts that are not themselves factorially unidimensional (e.g., Christie & Geis, 1970). Finally, as already stated, the program I propose would make sense only if the variables chosen had the potential to combine in some way so that they would form a system that predicted behavior more powerfully than the variables in the system considered singly. Allport (1937) pointed out long ago that factor analysis has little to say about the integration process.

Although I do not rule out the importance of previous factor analytic work in personality, I do suggest that before research be conducted, we attempt to establish which traits or other variables should be studied. These should be determined, for purposes of this minisystem by a group of experienced and creative personality psychologists who would form a group patterned after the vision research group.

Although the personality variables, unlike the vision variables, might not be chosen on the basis of a well-grounded theory, there would be theoretical work involved in choosing the variables. Furthermore, once empirical work began, theory would emerge.

A question that may arise is why focus on only a *few* variables. I suggest studying a few concepts in depth to maximize richness and minimize complexity of the system. Eysenck's success, although limited, attests to the usefulness of such an approach.

Is there a dependent variable or set of dependent variables central enough to serve in the proposed endeavor? Experimental personality research usually is not defined in terms of dependent variables but of independent variables. Contrast this, for example, to the situation in social psychology in which the problems are often defined in terms of dependent variables: attitude change, attraction, and so forth. The committee working on this problem would undoubtedly play a central role in making the decision about dependent variables. As is the case in vision, a single dependent variable might be chosen as central, but each investigator might be left free to study others. It may be premature to suggest a dependent variable. The choice of dependent variable(s) is, after all, intimately connected with the choice of independent variables. Since no independent variable or set of independent variables will predict everything, one cannot delineate an appropriate set of dependent variables without knowning the independent variables.

I do not believe that the suggested system would be a panacea for the field of personality or that it would provide a complete description of personality or do anything of the sort. The system instituted in vision unified an entire field, brought together investigators from a wide variety of disciplines, and had wide ramifications for theoretical advancement and for practical application. I would be satisfied if the project I propose simply advances the field of personality theoretically and empirically. With luck, the community of scholars in personality would realize some of the aims of the community of scholars in vision.

The important point is for experimental personality research to move beyond the typical research strategy in which a single individual difference concept is related to a series of dependent variables, to a more powerful strategy that utilizes several interacting constructs as predictors and has the potential of leading to a *system* of personality (cf. McGuire, 1973).

That the approach might indeed yield a system constitutes the answer to the last issue I wish to raise. The argument has been made (Ruch & Zimbardo, 1971, p. 439) that trait approaches to personality have offered no insight into personality organization or structure. However, I believe that if we approached the matter creatively, using the kind of scheme discussed here, we might learn a great deal about structure. There are at least two principles that may be relevant to the issue of structure: trait interaction (but cf. Zedeck, 1971), and the addition and subtraction of trait or traitlike variables (cf. Winter & Stewart, 1978). I wouldn't be surprised if unforeseen principles of interrelating personality concepts arose once the proposed project got underway. It would, of course, be crucial to come to terms with the theory *underlying* the principles.

This paper has advocated two strategies for personality research: First, integrate biological variables into experimental personality research, and second, attack the problem of the personality system. These suggestions need not be separate. Indeed, taken together they may suggest a new grand theory of personality, as rich as the old theories but more rigorous and more precise.

REFERENCES

Allport, G. W. *Personality: A psychological interpretation.* New York: Holt, 1937.

Barker, R. G. *Ecological psychology.* Stanford: Stanford University Press, 1968.

Bowers, K. S. Situationism in psychology: An analysis and a critique. *Psychological Review,* 1973, *80,* 307-336.

Brody, N. *Personality.* New York: Academic Press, 1972.

Carlson, R. Personality. *Annual Review of Psychology,* 1975, *26,* 393-411.

Cattell, R. B. *The scientific analysis of personality.* Baltimore: Penguin, 1965.

Christie, R., & Geis, F. L. (Eds.). *Studies in Machiavellianism.* New York: Academic Press, 1970.

Dahlstrom, W. G. *Personality systematics and the problem of types.* Morristown, N.J.: General Learning Press, 1972.

Ekehammar, B. Interactionism in personality from a historical perspective. *Psychological Bulletin,* 1974, *81,* 1026-1048.

Endler, N. S., & Magnusson, D. (Eds.). *Interactional psychology and personality.* Washington: Hemisphere, 1976.

Festinger, L., Riecken, H. W., & Schachter, S. *When prophecy fails.* New York: Harper, 1956.

Festinger, L., Schachter, S., & Back, K. *Social pressures in informal groups.* New York: Harper, 1950.

Goldberg, L. R. *Toward a taxonomy of traits.* Unpublished report. Eugene, Ore.: Oregon Research Institute, 1977.

Golding, S. L. Flies in the ointment: Methodological problems in the analysis of percent of variance due to persons and situations. *Psychological Bulletin,* 1975, *82,* 278-288.

Guilford, J. P. *Personality.* New York: McGraw-Hill, 1959.

Kelly, E. L. *Assessment of human characteristics.* Belmont, Calif.: Brooks/Cole, 1967.

Kuhn, T. S. *The structure of scientific revolutions.* Chicago: University of Chicago Press, 1962.

Leary, T. *Interpersonal diagnosis of personality.* New York: Ronald, 1957.

London, H., & Exner, J. (Eds.). *Dimensions of personality.* New York: Wiley, 1978.

Magnusson, D., & Endler, N. S. *Personality at the crossroads.* 1977.

Marlowe, D., & Gergen, K. J. Personality and social interaction. In G. Lindzey and E. Aronson (Eds.), *Handbook of social psychology.* Reading, Mass.: Addison-Wesley, 1969.

McGuire, W. J. The yin and yang of progress in social psychology: Seven koan. *Journal of Personality and Social Psychology,* 1973, *26,* 446-456.

Mischel, W. Toward a cognitive social learning reconceptualization of personality. *Psychological Review,* 1973, *80,* 252-283.

Mischel, W. *Introduction to personality.* New York: Holt, 1976.

National Research Council, Assembly of Behavioral and Social Sciences,

Committee on Vision. *First interprofessional standard for visual field testing.* Washington: National Academy of Sciences, 1975.

Norman, W. T. Toward an adequate taxonomy of personality attributes: Replicated factor structure in peer nomination personality ratings. *Journal of Abnormal and Social Psychology,* 1963, *66,* 574–583.

Overall, J. Note on the scientific status of factors. *Psychological Bulletin,* 1964, *61,* 270–276.

Pappenheimer, J. Standardization of definition and symbols in respiratory physiology. *Federation Proceedings,* 1950, *9,* 602–605.

Ruch, F. L., & Zimbardo, P. G. *Psychology and life* (8th ed.). Glenview, Ill.: Scott, Foresman, 1971.

Sarason, I. G., Smith, R. E., & Diener, E. Personality research: Components of variance attributable to the person and the situation. *Journal of Personality and Social Psychology,* 1975, *32,* 199–204.

Schachter, S. *The psychology of affiliation.* Stanford, Calif.: Stanford University Press, 1959.

Schachter, S. *Emotion, obesity, and crime.* New York: Academic Press, 1971.

Schachter, S., & Rodin, J. (Eds.). *Obese humans and rats.* Hillsdale, N.J.: Erlbaum, 1974.

Schutz, W. C. *FIRO-B.* Palo Alto, Calif.: Consulting Psychologists Press, 1967.

Secunda, S. K. The depressive disorders. Washington: U.S. Government Printing Office, 1973.

Wilson, G. Introversion/extraversion. In H. London & J. Exner (Eds.), *Dimensions of personality.* New York: Wiley, 1978.

Winter, D. G., & Stewart, A. J. The power motive. In H. London & J. Exner (Eds.), *Dimensions of personality.* New York: Wiley, 1978.

Zedeck, S. Problems with the use of "moderator" variables. *Psychological Bulletin,* 1971, *76,* 295–310.

AUTHOR INDEX

SUBJECT INDEX